The Beauty of a Diamond

through the eyes of a coach

Dan Clouser

ISBN: 1468145673
ISBN 13: 9781468145670

Library of Congress Control Number: 2012900039
CreateSpace, North Charleston, SC

Chapters

About The Author

*D*an Clouser founded the Berkshire Baseball Club, a nonprofit youth baseball organization that is based in Reading, Pennsylvania in 1989. He still serves as the organizations President and General Manager today.

The organization was founded on the basic principles of teaching young people life lessons through the game of baseball. The organization encourages the beliefs of good sportsmanship, honesty, loyalty, dignity, humility, class and respect for authority.

In addition, the organization stresses the importance of community service, volunteerism and giving back to the community.

Clouser also founded the organizations Scholarship Fund, which has awarded over $30,000 in scholarships since its inception in 2001 as well as the organizations World Equipment Outreach Program in 2006, which has donated over five-hundred boxes and counting of baseball and softball equipment to children in need throughout the world.

Clouser's coaching career has lasted for 23 years and counting. During that tenure, he has coached over 1,300 games at several different age levels and has left an indelible mark on the lives of the players that he has coached.

Clouser has also served as an associate scout for the Philadelphia Phillies since 2001.

He has dedicated his life to giving back and helping others.

Acknowledgements

Front & Back Cover Photography . . . . Stephen & Sherry Croft

Cover Design and Photo Enhancement . . . . Tara Gouck

Editing . . . . .Gail Cato

Additional Photo Credits:
Jim Minisce, Stephen Croft, Sherry Croft, Robert Jordan, Hope Distasio
& Carl Fischer.

*Cover Photo taken at FirstEnergy Stadium, America's Classic Ballpark, home
of the Reading Phillies, AA Eastern League Affiliate of the Philadelphia Phillies.*

I'd like to thank Scott Hunsicker, Dan Douglas and Matt Hoffmaster
of the Reading Phillies for allowing me to use your beautiful facility
for this book cover. Thanks again to Stephen & Sherry Croft for your
photography work and Tara Gouck for designing an awesome cover
concept and photo enhancement.

Special Thanks

This project was a 9 year work in progress, during that time, I had many people in my corner helping and supporting me throughout the process.

I'd like to thank my family first and foremost. To my wife Sandy, thank you for always being there to support me in everything that I've ever done in my life, you're the love of my life, my soul mate and my best friend. I would have never completed this project without you.

To my daughters, Sherry Croft, Kelly Capriolo and Stephanie Lingle thank you for always being there and understanding who I am. To my son James, you're still in my heart.

To my father for instilling strong beliefs and values in me, showing me the right way to do things and always keeping me in line.

To my mother, you contributed to everything that is in this book and more in one form or another. You and Dad have molded me into the man that I am today.

To my brother, Don, thanks for watching over me for all of those years and being my best friend.

To Steve Degler and Mike Billera-Smith, thanks for taking an early look, providing feedback and always asking me when it would be done.

To Jeff Potter, thanks for making me face that fear of failure and forcing me to make a commitment to this project.

I'd like to especially thank all of the players, parents and families who have touched my life through the game of baseball over the course of the last twenty-plus years, you have all made an indelible mark on my life and I will never forget you. This book is about you, each and every one of you who have touched my life.

Dedication

Loretta Magary,
The Wind Beneath My Wings

I had started writing this book in 2003; obviously, it has been somewhat of a work in progress. When I first started kicking around the idea of writing it, my mother was one of the first to step up and encourage me to go ahead with it. Since that time, my mother has passed away, so I feel that it is only fitting, now that I have finally finished this project, that I dedicate it to her.

Below is an article I wrote that appeared in the Berkshire Baseball and Softball Club's program booklet in 2005. I hope that by reading this, you may understand what has driven one individual to succeed beyond anyone's wildest dreams…

Since 1989 I have dedicated the bulk of my free time to the Berkshire Baseball and Softball Club, my wife can vouch for that. On days when I get a little overwhelmed and frustrated, and I ask myself what drives me, the answer is simply my mother and the kids who are in the program. Ever since I can remember, my mother volunteered her time in one form or another. Whether it was at the Little League concession stand when I was a kid or at the Salvation Army tent at ground zero; she always saw fit to lend a helping hand. In many cases, when I was younger, she would drag me along with her. Apparently, those days must have made a lasting impression on me. Quite honestly, I really can't think of anything that I would have rather done over the past twenty-three years than put in the time that I have with this organization, seeing young men grow into adulthood, and hoping that somewhere along the line, I may have helped them to achieve their goals.

Enough about me though, this article is dedicated to the person who taught me that there is no greater gift than to give of yourself. She lived her life by that motto, and I hope that my life can have half of the impact on others that hers did.

January 21, 2005, was the most painful day that I have ever experienced in my life. Getting the phone call from Florida that my mother was rushed into emergency open-heart surgery was tough; getting the phone call five hours later, telling me that she didn't make it through the surgery was a pain that I can't even put into words. My mother had such an incredible influence on my life that I feel I have to share it with others.

My mother—where do I begin? She was, by far, the most extraordinary woman that I have ever met. Although my heart aches and longs to see her smile just one more time, I am also so very proud of the things my mom accomplished in her short life, things that most people only ever dream of doing.

She was a Gypsy, a volunteer, a great teacher, and a mentor all in one.

The Gypsy in her, traveled around the country at her own pace and on her own terms. I can still remember when she first told me that she was going to quit her job to go see the United States in an old beat-up car; she later graduated to an old beat-up camper. My first reaction was that she had lost it. When she reasoned with me that many people travel all around the world to see different places and die without ever realizing what a beautiful country we live in right here and that she didn't want to be one of those people, how could I possibly argue with her? Not that I would have changed her mind anyway; she was determined once she made her mind up.

As I received letters from her telling me about her adventures, my admiration grew greater and greater for her. She saw every state in the union except Hawaii. She would stop to see family and friends along the way. When she ran low on cash, she would settle down with a friend or relative and work pumping gas or doing some other odd job until she had enough money saved up to continue.

I guess in a way, the Gypsy in her has rubbed off on me as well; however, I have chosen to see our great country with fifty-plus teenage baseball players in tow. She saw it by herself in a 1967 Plymouth Valiant and later in a 1978 Toyota camper.

The volunteer in her made her the most giving person I have ever met. I can remember growing up in Florida. After she and my father had separated and it was just my mother and me; she worked two, three, and sometimes four jobs to make ends meet. I know now that things were pretty tough for us, but I never knew it then. She made sure we always had food on the table and a roof over our heads. She took a backseat to make sure I was taken care of. She would take me shopping for school clothes at the mall and we'd stop at Goodwill for herself on the way home.

Even with working all those jobs, she seldom ever missed a Little League game and always made sure I was at practice.

She continued giving of herself long after I was gone. Whether it was at ground zero after 9/11, in Florida with hurricane relief efforts, helping a friend stay sober, volunteering with the Florida attorney general's rape crisis network, or just helping a friend put shingles on his roof, she always had time to lend a hand. She would seldom ask for help but was always ready to give it. Always looking out for everyone else that even in her last days, she didn't want her parents or brothers and sisters to know she was in the hospital because she didn't want them to worry about her. Even in her death, she was still looking out for someone else; as an organ donor, she gave, among other things, the tissue of her corneas. My Aunt Sally said it best when she said she wishes that whoever gets them can see the beauty that my Mom saw with them.

The career that she chose was as giving as her volunteer duties. She was an addictions counselor and ran a halfway house for several years. She was very active in Alcoholics Anonymous and Al-Anon.

The teacher in her taught me so many things, that I can only highlight a few…

She taught me that people are still people whether they are famous or not. She stressed that after all the fame and fortune goes away, the type of person you are is how others will remember you.

She held hands with Jim McMahon of the Chicago Bears in "Hands across America" and was not very impressed by him. She had lunch with Dickie Noles of the 1980 World Champion Philadelphia Phillies every year at an annual convention in Clearwater, Florida, and referred to him as "a nice southern kid who *did* mention something about playing baseball a few times." She was very impressed with him, telling me that he was the "real deal."

Obviously, she taught me how to be a volunteer and give of myself.

She taught me how important family is. Whether it's full blood, half blood, or marriage, my mom taught me that family is family and that's just the way it was. No matter what she had going on, she made sure she always made the trek from Florida to Pennsylvania to get to her grandchildren's high school and college graduations. She had both biological grandchildren and step grandchildren, but referred to them all as her grandchildren—period.

She taught me that God requires me, as a parent, to teach my children only two things: how to walk and how to walk away, and that the second requirement is a whole lot tougher than the first.

She taught me that living your life with the Serenity Prayer as a motto is a pretty good thing.

The day my mother died, I was at a baseball coaches' clinic in Cherry Hill, New Jersey. One of the speakers, Pat McMahon, was the head coach at the University of Florida and I have gotten to know him very well over the past few years. He ended his segment by giving us a quiz, and he asked us to answer two sets of questions...

The first set was to name the three richest people in the world, name the last three Heisman Trophy winners, and name the last three Super Bowl Champions.

The second set of questions was to name three family members, name three friends, and name three people who have taught you something.

After we all had our answers, he asked for a show of hands as to who had all nine names filled in on the first list. In a room of close to three hundred people, not one hand came up.

He then asked for a show of hands as to who had nine names on the second list. Every hand in the room came up.

The moral of his story is that after all the fame, fortune, and accolades, people will quickly forget about you. However, the second list is a list that can stand the test of time. Family, friends, and teachers will be with you forever, and as coaches, we should strive to get on every one of our players' second lists.

My mother was at the top of all three of my lists for the second set of questions.

She lived her life to the fullest, she had no regrets. She touched the lives of so many people, it's impossible to fathom.

It was stunning to have so many people that I had never met before, come up to me at her memorial service or send us a letter after her death telling me that my mom "saved their life" or impacted their life in some way.

She always had a unique outlook on life, she could find something good in everyone, but was never afraid to tell you when you screwed up either.

I will miss her dearly, but thank God that I had her for a mother.

She is still my hero and will always be the "Wind beneath My Wings."

CHAPTER 1

The Diamond Teaches Life Lessons

*M*ost people, when they see the cover and title of this book, will immediately think that it's a book about baseball, which it is; however, more importantly, it's a book about life.

Baseball has been the one constant in my life for as long as I can remember. It was the first organized sport that I ever played. It has made me joyous and it has broken my heart. It has been my best friend and my worst enemy. I have met thousands of friends through my involvement in this game, people who I love and cherish to this day.

Baseball has become the thread of my life. Most of the people who know me, know that baseball plays an extremely large role in whom and what I have become in this world. A few years back, my cousin, Paul Wade, III had passed away at just the age of 35. The team that I was coaching at the time was playing a doubleheader in Wilmington, Delaware, which was only about an hour from where my uncle lived in

Yardley, Pennsylvania. As opposed to driving back to Reading after our games and heading back out to Yardley to spend some time with my family, I had decided that it made more sense for me to drive separately from the team and go right to Yardley from Wilmington. Because I had left right after our second game, I was still in my uniform when I arrived in Yardley at my uncle's house, and several of my other aunts, uncles, and cousins were already there. I remember my cousin Carole telling me that she always remembered me wearing a baseball uniform. I didn't think much of it at the time, but now, as I reflect back, I realize just how that statement alone proves how much of a role baseball has played in my life.

The biggest thing I realize though is that baseball has been the tool or the avenue that has opened so many other doors in my life. Baseball has not defined me as an individual; however, it has allowed me to do more things and meet more people than I could have ever imagined. Some people find that difficult to understand. Early in my life, it was about the game of baseball itself, but as I have grown, I have realized that the game itself plays a very small part in what I have been fortunate enough to experience as a human being. However, baseball has been the one common thread, the one tool, the one constant that has allowed everything else to take place.

Most of all, baseball has taught me lessons in life that I use every day. I have always been able to understand the game of baseball. That understanding came very naturally for me. There are well-defined guidelines and principles that must be followed to play the game. Life, on the other hand, has not always been that easy for me to understand. To be able to relate baseball to real life has helped me incredibly throughout my years. As a coach, I can only hope that helping my players understand life through the game of baseball will be my ultimate gift to them.

Sometimes, I will use the game as an escape from the everyday craziness that life can bring. Coaching baseball and playing baseball have always provided a very safe haven for me. Between those white lines, I can control the things that happen for the most part. The rules of the game and the way you go about your business on the field are very well defined. In life, that is not always the case, but as I said before, baseball has certainly helped me to understand some of the unexpected curves that life can throw at you.

Baseball has provided that safe haven for me for a long time. Whenever things were going badly, there was never any better place for me to be than at the ballpark. When I was younger and my parents were going through a divorce, the ballpark always seemed to provide some type of solace that I couldn't get anywhere else. As I grew older, the ballpark remained that one constant where everything was always OK.

There didn't even have to be a game going on. Just sitting in the bleachers of an empty ballpark has always provided me with an incredible sense of peace. Even now, after a bad day at work or if my wife and I are fighting, nothing can clear my head like just sitting and staring at a baseball field. Empty or full of action, it doesn't matter to me; hot summer day or covered with snow in the dead of winter, it still provides an incredible sense of relaxation.

I heard someone once say that a bad day at the ballpark is still better than most good days anywhere else. I can certainly relate to that.

So how has baseball taught me about life? Pretty simple—baseball is a game of adjustments, just as life is a game of adjustments. If you're thinking fastball, and life throws you a curve, you have to make the adjustment or you'll look silly.

Baseball has taught me that like life, how you react to every situation has a bearing, either positive or negative on you and those around you. It has taught me to keep my composure, regardless of the situation. Keep your emotions in check and never lose focus of the goal. Regardless of what happened today, the sun will come up tomorrow.

As a baseball coach, I look at the responsibility that I have to my players both on and off the field as my legacy. I have coached teams that have consisted of players thirteen and fourteen years old and I have coached teams that have consisted of collegiate-age players as well as every age in between. I approach them all the same way.

I want to teach them about the game of baseball, how to hit a curve ball, how to throw a curve ball, how to field, how to run the bases, how to hit and run, and steal a base.

Most of all, I feel that I have an obligation to my players to teach them life's lessons through the game. Teamwork, controlling your emotions, treating your opponents and teammates with respect, dealing with failure, being proud, yet humble, these are all things that baseball will teach you.

Teaching by your example to instill a burning desire into every one of them to be successful; both individually and as a team. Making them aware of how their actions affect themselves and their teammates, and teaching them to take responsibility for those actions.

Making them understand that no matter how good a baseball player they are, that at some point, the game will pass them by. Baseball is kind of cruel in that sense. It will take everything you have to offer and when you have nothing left to offer, it simply moves onto to the next guy. For some players, that time will be after their high school seasons end; for some others it may be following college; those more talented can go on to play the game professionally, maybe even end up in the Hall of Fame. However, regardless of how good you are, at some point your body says it's time to move on and the game will brush by you like the wind. It's at that point in your life where there has to be something of substance inside of you. You have to be sincere and genuine. Once you get into the real world, it doesn't matter how hard you could throw a fastball or how far you could hit one; people can identify a jackass from a mile away. Whether you were famous or just an average Joe, you have to have some type of substance inside. Some very famous people have ended their careers and hit rock bottom because they realized that what they had at the end of the day was nothing—no true friends, maybe some leftover money, but for the most part, a very empty and lonely life outside of the limelight.

For that reason alone, I preach to all of my players that they must take life seriously. Whether it's on the baseball field, in the classroom, or in the workforce, you have to put your best foot forward. You don't get a second chance and it can be too late before you even know it.

I have been very fortunate to meet several professional and former professional baseball players in my life. I'm not talking about walking past them in spring training and getting an autograph, I mean actually talking to them, having dinner with them, driving with them in my truck.

As president of the Berkshire Baseball and Softball Club, an organization that I started in 1989, I enjoy perks of the position such as scheduling the guest speakers for our annual scholarship and awards banquet. After scheduling them, I normally get to speak with them on the phone once or twice, have lunch or dinner with them, and pick them up at the airport. All that sort of good stuff falls within my realm of responsibility. Most of them have been very genuine people: Dickie Noles, Eric Valent, Al Oliver, Goose Gossage, Mike Easler, Bernie Carbo, John Morris, Billy Ripken, Bill "Spaceman" Lee, Ozzie Virgil Jr., and Ron LeFlore are just a few that I have met. I am very proud that I have been able to spend some time with them. They were all very humble and I learned a lot from each of them. Some of them have even told me that they learned something from me. Now isn't that something?

I have also met several that don't deserve mention here. Guys who felt that the world owed them something just because they wore a professional uniform and that I should have felt honored just to be in their presence and have them speak to me. Needless to say, I wasn't impressed. They were fakes and I could see right through them.

I first met Dickie Noles while working a baseball camp back in 2000. Even though I am an adult, I get as excited as a five-year-old kid when I get the chance to meet a big league player or a former big leaguer. Meeting Dickie was no different for me. I got to spend a lot of time with him the day we worked together. It was awesome listening to his stories and seeing how he genuinely wanted to make a difference in the lives of the kids he spoke to. When the camp was over I was on cloud nine, so when I got home, I did what any other thirty-something-year-old man would have done. I called my mom to tell her that I had met Dickie Noles that day.

My eyes were opened incredibly during the conversation, which went like this, "Hey, Mom, you'll never guess who I met today!"

She replied, "Who?"

I said, "Guess…"

She said, "Really, I have no idea, so why don't you just tell me."

So I finally gave in and exclaimed, "Dickie Noles!"

Her reply, simply floored me, "Dickie Noles? I know Dickie Noles," she said.

I paused and replied, "You mean you know who Dickie Noles is, right? You've heard the name before. He played for the Philadelphia Phillies." I was quite surprised that my mom even recognized the name because, quite frankly, unlike me, she was not much of a baseball fan. I mean she enjoyed the game and never missed one of my games and never had any issues with taking me to a spring training game when I was a kid, but to actually know a player's name was a little bit shocking to me to say the least.

"I'm not sure about all that, I guess he played baseball, I think I remember him saying that he played baseball," she said. "But I do *know* him; I have lunch with him every year. He's a very nice young southern boy, right?"

"Dickie Noles?" I again said in bewilderment. "He played for the Phillies. He was on the 1980 Philadelphia Phillies World Championship team with Mike Schmidt, Steve Carlton, Tug McGraw…what exactly do you mean you *know* him?"

"Just what I said, I have lunch with him every year in Clearwater at an addictions counselor's convention. He is a super young man and I think he once mentioned that he played baseball," she calmly explained to me."

Baffled, I sat silently on the phone for a few minutes.

Once I gathered myself and realized that the name Dickie Noles couldn't really be confused and that my mother, who knew and cared very little about baseball, really had no reason to try to impress me by untruthfully telling that she knew Dickie Noles.

With nothing else to say, my only response was, "Wow, why didn't you tell me you knew Dickie Noles?"

Her response was simple, yet it proved to me what I had been trying to teach my players for so many years. My mother, as only a mother could do, taught me an even greater life lesson than I could teach my players, when she simply said, "I guess I just didn't think it was that big of a deal, I don't tell you about any other lunches that I have."

So there it was, plain and simple, cut and dry. In my mother's eye's, Dickie Noles was a great, genuine, and caring human being. A fellow addictions counselor who she had a great deal of admiration and respect for, but most importantly, someone she considered as a friend and colleague.

The fact Dickie Noles helped the Philadelphia Phillies accomplish what at that time was their only World Championship meant absolutely nothing to my mother. The fact that he was successful on baseball's greatest stage, again, meant nothing to Loretta Magary. The only thing that mattered to my mom was that Dickie was a good person. Nothing more, nothing less. She didn't need to know that he had won a World Championship to figure that out.

I always tell my players to never forget where they came from. I think that is always the beginning of the end for you as a person. Once you have forgotten where you came from and forget those who helped you get to where you're at, it's pretty much all over at that point.

Everyone in this world has had someone who has helped them at some point. We can't always go back to those people who helped us along the way and pay them back, but I have always felt that if you share some of that knowledge with others, it is just as much of an honor. That's the real payback—knowing that when you start to give, you will receive nothing in return, but hoping that what you give keeps giving.

That was one of the many things my mother taught me. She said as she got older and started doing more and more volunteer work, that that was payback time for everyone who had ever helped her.

My aunt asked her one time why she spent so much time volunteering, helping other people, and never seeming like she wanted anything in return. My mother, as only she could do, just said, "I have gone through some very tough times in my life, there have been many people who have helped me out along the way, so for me now, it's just payback time."

I guess that's my goal. That's the greatest honor that any of my former players will ever be able to give me. Years after I am gone, for a former player of mine to move on into coaching and to say to his players, "An old coach of mine once taught me this…"

That will be payback time. I am working toward that as a legacy. I want to teach my players about life through the game of baseball and then see them go on and teach their players about life through the game of baseball in return. There would truly be no greater gift in the world.

CHAPTER 2

Learning Teamwork Through The Game

I was never fortunate enough to fulfill not only my, but just about every other American boy's childhood dream of playing the game I love professionally. However, that has never curbed my desire to stay involved with this game as long as I possibly can.

I was never a great player; I had to bust my ass for every inning that I ever got on the field. I worked hard in practice and always hustled. Being part of a team was very important to me even at a very young age and I think that is something that has helped me tremendously both personally and professionally. I think that teamwork is one of the most important aspects that baseball and softball bring to the table. It's a pretty simple fact of life that if you can't be a team player, you're going to struggle. That's a fact that goes far beyond the playing field. No matter what you do in life, you're going to be part of a team. In business, it doesn't matter if you're the CEO or the guy that sweeps the floor; at the end of the day, you're part of a team. This concept is so simple, yet so hard to grasp for some people.

Look at it this way, the CEO of a multimillion dollar company can be the smartest, most competent and aggressive businessperson around, however, if the person that sweeps the floor isn't a team player and doesn't take pride in the job, guess what? The first impression that the public gets when they walk into that building is from the guy sweeping the floor, not the CEO. If a client walks through that door and sees a dirty office building, the CEO's job just got that much tougher. That's teamwork, that's a fact.

So whether it's in the business world or your personal life, you're going to be part of a team. Marriage is a lifelong commitment to teamwork. Even if you're single, you're still part of a team, your family. It's constantly teamwork. No matter where you turn in life, you're going to see that teamwork is prevalent.

I've had this conversation with many people in my lifetime and a common response is, "Well, yes, I agree, but teamwork exists in every sport, not just baseball." Although that is a true statement, it's not *really* the same in other sports. Baseball and softball are the only sports that represent *true* teamwork.

Take this for instance: the game is on the line, closing minutes. In football, the coach is going to design a play that will get the ball into his best playmakers' hands. The same thing is going to happen in basketball, hockey, soccer, you name it. Game on the line; get it to the guy or girl who has the best percentages working in your favor.

In baseball or softball, that's not the case. Bottom of the ninth, bases loaded, two outs, your team down by a run, the league's best closer on the mound—guess who steps to the plate—your number nine hitter who is 0-for-4 on the day with two strikeouts and bringing a .220 average to the plate. Here's the coach's decision: do I roll the dice with the number nine hitter or do I go to a pinch hitter who last swung a bat five hours ago in batting practice and has a stiff butt from sitting on the bench for the last three hours? Now that's teamwork. In baseball or softball in that situation, the coach can't call a timeout and move his number four hitter into that situation because he's the guy who is 4-for-4 with three RBI's already today. That's the difference, that's where your true colors come shining through, and that is true teamwork. The old phrase that states that a chain is only as strong as its weakest link—that's baseball.

Everything that nine guys have worked together for, oftentimes comes down to one play, one instance, one time when that number nine hitter slaps a Texas leaguer over the shortstop's head and finishes the game 1-for-5 with one RBI. He's the guy with the headline in tomorrow's paper, he's the guy you watch on *Sports Center* that night, that number four hitter who had the three RBIs, he's now the afterthought. Once again, that is the true spirit of teamwork. Teamwork even for the number four hitter who knows that if old number nine comes through he loses the limelight but who also realizes that if old number nine doesn't come through, neither of them gets the headline.

A professional baseball team can have the two best pitchers in the game and have nothing to show for it at the end of the season. Those top two guys can go out and win twenty-five games each, but if the other three guys can muster up only ten wins each, guess what? You're four games below .500 at the end of the season. Once again, any other sport, all of the best guys are out there *every* night, not every *fifth* night. A football quarterback doesn't play every fifth game nor does your best point guard. But that's baseball, that's the true essence of teamwork. Your number five starter is going to face the best lineup in the league sometime during the season, your worst fielder is going to have a ball hit to him, and your worst hitter is still going step in the box four times a night. When those cases arise, teamwork comes shining through. The other eight guys know that they have to score two more runs to win, they know they're going to have to get a little dirtier on defense and they know that they have to make sure that the guy who may not have the best stuff on the mound knows that he can depend on them as well. They have to give him the extra confidence to go out and give it a 110 percent and under no circumstances can they ever make him feel as if they don't believe in him.

This game is a game of failure. If you fail 70 percent of the time at the professional level, they might hang a bronze plaque of your face on a wall in Cooperstown. Do the same in college, you might get a chance to play at the next level, do it in high school, and it's all the same. That again, though, is the true essence of the teamwork that baseball represents. If you fail 70 percent of the time, your teammates will rally around you and raise their game as well.

That's what I mean when I talk about teamwork, on the baseball field. It is nine different individuals working for the same common goal in a game. It is twenty-five different individuals, who know their roles working for one common goal for the entire season. In the business world, it is the largest corporation with thousands of employees working for that same common goal; it is the smallest mom-and-pop store on the corner with two or three employees working for that same common goal. In the family, it is moms and dads and sons and daughters all working together.

All it takes is one person who loses sight of that goal, one person who thinks he or she is better than the team, one person to drop the ball; one person with a negative attitude and the whole thing can come crumbling down. That again is the essence of teamwork. Teamwork is something that takes work. Every day an obstacle is going to present itself to you, and when you can stick together as a team—whether in the baseball world or anywhere else in life—that is when you will overcome and be successful. Anyone can walk away; anyone can throw in the towel; that's the easy way out. Pulling together as a team when things start to look darkest is what will show your true human spirit.

I often refer to the two-horse rule when trying to make my players understand how important teamwork is. I once read that a single horse can pull six tons by itself. However, add another horse pulling in the same direction and they can pull thirty-six tons together. Six times what they can pull on their own. A simply amazing illustration of what real teamwork can really do in its own right. I then like to go on and add two other scenarios. Take those same two horses and their original six-ton load, face them in opposite directions, and see how far they get. Teamwork isn't just the shear adding of numbers to the task, it's those numbers all pulling in the same direction, being on the same page, if you will. The numbers alone, if all pulling in separate directions will go nowhere. Lastly, I like to add the fact that if the two horses can pull six times what they can pull on their own, just think of what we as a team of fifteen, sixteen, twenty, twenty-five, or whatever the case may be, can pull if we're all on the same page and pulling in the same direction. The possibilities of what we as a team can accomplish are endless.

Even some of the experiences on the field are tough to explain to someone who has never experienced it firsthand. It is just so difficult to put into words. When I watch the Super Bowl or final game of a

World Series and see grown men cry after they win, I can completely understand why they do. I have sat with people who have actually said to me that they can't understand why a grown man would cry over a game. The people who say that have never been part of a team that has worked over an entire season to achieve a common goal.

To win a championship over the course of a season, whether you are a kid, a high school player, a college player, an amateur, or a professional, it still means the same thing to you when you do it. The stages may all be different, but the feeling is the same. It is the culmination of months and months of hard work, blood, sweat, and tears. Fifteen, twenty, twenty-five guys all pulling together to achieve the same common goal. When that happens and you are a part of it, you completely understand how important every single member of that team is. People on the outside may not be able to comprehend what the last guy off the bench contributed, but his twenty-four teammates will certainly understand how important he is. Teams win championships—period. In this day and age you will see so many professional sports teams that go out and try to "buy" themselves a championship, it seldom works because those teams of superstars often lack the chemistry that it takes to win a championship. Twenty-five individuals do not win championships, twenty-five teammates do. I once heard Bobby Bowden say that he tries to teach his players how to love each other. He was referring to the love of brothers and that a team that loves each other is a tough team to beat.

This again is something that is difficult for someone who does not have a sibling to understand, but, for example, my brother, who is nine years older than I am, would make it his responsibility to kick the ever living crap out of me on a regular basis when we were kids. There were seriously times when I swear I was doing nothing other than walking past him and he would see fit to pop me for no apparent reason. From the outside, someone else may have thought that the two of us hated each other; however, if someone else ever wanted to mess with me when we were growing up, they would have to pay an awfully high price of having to get through Don Clouser before they could even touch his little brother. A few people tried to test that theory and the results were ugly, to be frank. As we grew up, my respect and admiration for my older brother never waned. We are two very different individuals but will back each other up all the time. He was the best man in my wedding, not because he was my older brother, but because he is truthfully my best friend.

So when you get a team together that takes on the philosophy that they are a "band of brothers," I mean guys who are really willing to take a bullet for each other, that is a team that is going to be tough to beat.

Every day of your life you're going to be presented with a way out. Every day you have to come back to the same question, "Should I stay or should I go?" It is willpower, pride, and teamwork that drive you to stay on course and achieve your goals.

No other sport represents real-life teamwork the way baseball does.

In 2007, the 16-U team that I had may have exemplified teamwork more than any other group that I had ever coached. This was a very special group of kids. The core group of that squad, Brandon Shurr, Nick Riegel, Phil Anderson, Willie Schaeffer, Brock Laubenstine, and Tyler Deshong, were returning from our 2006 squad. That returning core had a very vivid memory of a heartbreaking 11-9 loss in Las Vegas that ended their previous season and dashed their hopes of advancing to the quarterfinals of the LVBA Desert Fall Classic 16-U Division. We added to that solid core of six players with Ty Frick, Mark Minisce, Dylan Mazzo, Jimmy Davis, Ryan Buday, Ryan Brennan, Kevin O'Neill, Matt Turman, and Jordan Gottshall. At the beginning of the season, we looked extremely solid on paper. We had great pitching, defense, speed, and solid hitting. We knew as a coaching staff that this team could do some special things.

In their first tournament, the club advanced to the semifinals of the Kinteco Mid-Summer Classic, only to lose a tough 7-6 game in ten innings.

The next tournament, the Grand Slam Pretzel City Classic, we again advanced to the semifinals, only to lose 7-5 to the Southeastern Pennsylvania Pirates.

Our next tournament, the kids played very good baseball to advance to the Championship Game of the Hooters Wood Bat Classic. The championship game of the tournament ended up being postponed by rain, and it didn't resume for more than two weeks.

During that two weeks we went a disappointing 1-2 at the Sports at the Beach Challenge of Champions in Rehoboth Beach, Delaware, and we once again were tripped up in the semifinals of the Pagoda Classic by a 5-4, eleven-inning loss to our rival, the PlayBall Stars.

Once we finally made that Hooters title game appearance, we came out flat and lost 3-0 to the Harrisburg Pioneers.

The team continued to struggle in big games. As a coaching staff, we were searching for answers and a way to get the most out of this talented yet underachieving group.

Heading into our midway point of the season and getting ready for the White Star Fall Classic Tournament, we were sitting on a 10-10-1 record and were looking to shake the tag of being an average team.

With three pool play games scheduled for one day, we split our first two games of the day with an 11-1 win over the Devon Shockers and a 5-1 loss to Mid-Atlantic Regional powerhouse, the Tri-State Arsenal.

Heading into our final pool game of the day, we knew that we needed to beat our arch nemesis, the PlayBall Stars, again to advance to the elimination round on Sunday.

Heading into the bottom of the seventh inning, we had a 6-2 lead and things were looking pretty good.

After recording the first out of the inning, the wheels fell off and we blew the lead, as it seemed as though nothing could go right as the Stars scored five runs in the bottom of the seventh inning to win the game 7-6. The loss demoralized the team, as it seemed like we were on the brink all season long and just couldn't close the deal in the big games.

The next day, in a consolation game, we went out and pounded a very good Upper Salford Diamond Dogs club 12-0.

In our next game, we beat an 18-U team, the Berks County Wizards, 8-3, again by playing very good, fundamentally sound baseball.

Following the win against the Wizards, we decided to talk to the team about their approach to games. I told the squad that we needed to play more relaxed and start enjoying the game of baseball more. They needed to approach every game as if it meant absolutely nothing. Any pressure to perform that was being put on them—whether it was from their parents, us as coaches, or each other—they needed to completely ignore it and just go out and have fun every game. It seemed like when there was nothing on the line, they played very relaxed and did everything right. In weeknight exhibition games and pool games, they were awesome, making every play, throwing strikes, running the bases with style and grace. Then, when we would get to a semifinal or championship, we would just come out extremely tight and fall on our faces. I emphasized that we had to go into every game relaxed and just worry about having fun and playing the game.

The next night as we were getting ready for our game, my assistant coach, Brooke Kramer, Brandon Shurr, and I were sitting on the bench and goofing around with our pants. You see, my being a die-hard Boston Red Sox fan as well as the guy who orders our uniforms, I decided that our 16-U team would wear stirrups that season. Now these weren't just any stirrups, these were "old-school" Boston Red Sox stirrups; like the ones the Red Sox wore up until the 1970s that had the navy blue and white stripes around them. Up until this game, some kids would wear their pants down and some would put them up.

Brooke was commenting about how it was pointless to have the nifty little stirrups if half of the team was going to wear their pants down. So as we sat there, each of us, all of whom traditionally wore our pants down to the ankles, would pull our pants up to show off our stirrups. The two of them especially liked mine when they were pulled up, telling me that I looked like Babe Ruth. As other kids made their way to the bench from the batting cage, they decided to join in. As we all started to pull our pants up just messing around, Brooke suggested that we should all wear our pants up and show off our old-school socks as a sign of team unity. The kids bought into Brooke's idea and decided to give it a try. Although I still think that they all just liked seeing me look like Babe Ruth.

In their next tournament, the kids gelled like never before and we went 5-0-1 en route to our first tournament title of the season. Along the way, we found ways to win the same close games that we had been finding ways to lose all season long. Four of their five victories over that weekend, we won by one run, including two eight-inning games and a ten-inning game.

In the final, we took out the Tri-State Arsenal 7-6 to capture the title.

After another runner-up finish in the Rhino Cleaning Pink Ribbon Classic, we headed south to the Ripken Experience in Myrtle Beach, South Carolina, for our season finale.

Brock Laubenstine; whose father was in critical condition in the Reading Hospital's intensive care unit following a horrible truck accident the night before we left for Myrtle Beach, led the way for us as he cruised on the mound in our Friday night opener, a 12-2 win over the Chesapeake (Virginia) Bay Sox.

On Saturday, we took a split in our games, beating Longhorn (North Carolina) Baseball 12-5 and losing to the Carolina Thunder 5-1.

Going into Sunday, we needed to beat the Delaware Outlaws to have a shot at advancing to the title game.

Laubenstine, came back in relief of starter Brandon Shurr and got the win as we scored in the late innings to come from behind to win 6-5 and advance to the title game where we earned a rematch against the Thunder.

Jordan Gottshall started in the title game on the mound for us and pitched 5-1/3 solid innings. In the sixth, as we were clinging to a 4-3 lead, Gottshall struck out the lead-off hitter and then walked the next batter to give way to reliever, Jimmy Davis.

Davis fanned the first hitter he faced for the second out of the inning and then hit the next batter, the number nine hitter in the order, to put the tying run on second base and turn over the Thunder's order.

With a 1-0 count on the lead-off batter, a bizarre double-steal call ended the inning with our catcher, Tyler Deshong, gunning down the lead runner at third.

In the top of the seventh inning, we were looking for some insurance runs and Nick Riegel, who entered the game defensively in the bottom of the sixth, led off the inning by smoking a single into right field.

The Thunder then had trouble fielding Matt Turman's sacrifice bunt, which resulted in us having runners on first and second with no outs.

Ryan Buday then laid down another perfect bunt that the Thunder couldn't record an out on again and the ensuing error scored Riegel to put us up 5-3 and put runners on the corners.

Turman was then thrown out at the plate for the first out of the inning on an attempted first and third double-steal.

Shurr drew a walk to put runners on first and second, and Tyler Deshong loaded the bases on a throwing error by the Thunder second baseman.

Mark Minisce then hustled out an attempted double play, in which Buday scored on the fielder's choice, giving us a 6-3 lead.

Phil Anderson popped up to the third baseman to end the inning and make way for Laubenstine to make his second relief appearance of the day.

Facing the top of the Thunder's potent lineup in the bottom of the seventh, Laubenstine yielded a lead-off single and then got serious.

A fly out to center, a ground out to third, and a come backer to Laubenstine himself ended the inning and gave us a fitting end to a memorable season.

After we pulled our Socks up midway through the season, we went 22-6-1 on our way to an overall 33-18-2 mark, breaking our organization's 16-U single season win record, taking home two tournament titles and two runner-up finishes during the year.

Now we seriously know that there wasn't any type of magic potion when we decided to pull our pants up, but what it did was show that we were a team. We were on the same page from top to bottom. The kids gelled and they all accepted their roles. They were literally like brothers. They took a more relaxed approach after we pulled the pants up and they wouldn't let any pressure get to them. In fact, it almost seemed as though the more pressure of the situation, the better they played. Every single player on that fifteen-man roster came up with a huge hit, a huge defensive play, or an aggressive base running play at some point in the season. None of them cared if they started, if they came in from the bullpen, if they had a late inning pinch hit opportunity—it didn't matter. When they were called upon to help contribute to the team's success, they rose to the occasion and that is what made that group so special and so good that year. They were a team, they had one common goal, and every one of them would do whatever he was asked to do to help achieve that one goal.

CHAPTER 3

Winners Have Pride

*W*inners have pride. This is sometimes a difficult concept for people to understand as well. Not really to have pride, but what is pride? Pride is not arrogance or cockiness, pride is the burning desire deep inside your soul that pushes you to be the best that you can be.

When I was in sales for a building materials company, I achieved over $4.5 million dollars in sales during my best year. I earned a six-figure income and I was driven by nothing other than my own pride. It was just the simple pride, passion, and motivation to be the very best building materials sales representative that I could be that year. Money is not pride, although money can many times be a reward for pride. This is something that so many people lose sight of. Again, whether it is baseball or in your career, if you are not motivated simply by pride and the love of what you do, you will never be successful.

I strongly suggest that if you are in a career that you do not love, as so many Americans are, then get out. You will never be happy, regardless of how much money you may be making. Again, this is a very difficult concept for some people to grasp. However, I can tell you that if you are motivated for any reasons other than plain and simple self-pride, you will never end up being happy. What I mean by that is that when you are all alone at the end of the day and you look at yourself in the mirror, what do you see? That is the true test. You can lie to your boss, your wife, and your family, but you cannot lie to yourself. You cannot run from yourself. Only you can answer the one true test of a person's character.

Being in the sales field, I saw a lot of people who were motivated simply by the love of money. Although that type of motivation will work temporarily, you will find that it gets old very quick.

As I said earlier, my sole motivation was pride. I did everything in my power to satisfy my customers. Knowing that my customers knew they could depend on me is what drove me. They knew that if they gave me a project, it was going to get done. I never made a sale while calculating my commission, I seldom knew until the end of the month what my commission even was. That was not the driving force behind my motivation; it was simply the fruit of my motivation. If you don't take anything else to heart within these pages, please take that to heart. This one thing can truly change your life.

Even as a coach, my number one priority has never been winning. Now that may sound bizarre to many, but it is a fact. Winning was again the result of the pride that I took in being part of a team. The pride that I took in knowing what my responsibility was to the players that I coached. The one thing that you must understand is that all of my coaching experience has come in the youth and amateur baseball ranks. Something I learned very early on is that you are a part of a child's life for maybe three or four months over a spring, summer, or fall season but what you leave them with at the end of that season will last a lifetime for them, good or bad.

The pride that I took in knowing that I would have an everlasting impact on a player's life is what drove me to be successful as a coach. I have had the opportunity to coach some very good teams in my lifetime and I have had the opportunity to coach some very bad teams as well. I think I may have learned more as a human being while coaching the bad teams than I did while coaching the championship teams.

My first year coaching American Legion Baseball for the Conrad Weiser American Legion Baseball program in Robesonia, Pennsylvania,

I had the opportunity to take over a program that was on life support. We fielded a team of eleven kids, primarily of fifteen- and sixteen-year-olds to face a summer of being drubbed by eighteen-year-old studs. We finished 1-21 in what most people saw as a complete failure of a season. However, my assistant and I knew that the season was a huge success. In the beginning of the year, we had set a few very modest goals for ourselves. They were very simple. Number one, don't get anyone seriously injured. We couldn't afford to; we only had eleven players to begin with. This was established after our first practice and we realized that some of our players had very little experience actually playing baseball. Number two was to make sure that each player is better on the last day of the season than he was on the first. We accomplished both of the goals *and* we won a game.

Our next two years, we won twelve games each season and in my fourth and final year we won thirteen. We never did finish above .500, but I can feel confident when I say that just about every kid that went through that program in those four years was a better player when he left than when he started. That was the true success of my tenure with the Conrad Weiser American Legion baseball program. If my motivation were solely to win, I would have packed my bags immediately after that first year, maybe even after the first practice. So never lose sight of what should truly motivate you. Had I entered that position at Conrad Weiser with a bad attitude, the program may have died that first year.

As soon as I realized that this position would be a true test of my character, motivation, and love of the game. I realized that just because some of these kids were not very good baseball players, it didn't mean that they weren't good kids.

My years at Conrad Weiser were some of the only seasons in my life that I was ever part of a losing team. From Little League through high school and into adult amateur ball, I was always part of a winning or play-off team. Obviously, the Weiser experience was a trial by fire to see if I had what it took to look deeper into why we all should be coaching. We are truly here for the players, no other reason, regardless of how old they are. Whether it's Little League, high school, college, amateur, or professional coaching, your players will look to you for guidance both on and off the field. How you handle the pressure will directly reflect on how they handle the pressure.

I truly recommend to everyone who has ever coached, if you have never been part of a losing team, if you have done nothing other than win, to leave your current post, and then go out and find the worst team that you can find and coach there for a few years. People laugh when I say that. A friend of mine, Del Mintz, who is now a scout and my boss with the Philadelphia Phillies, who was cast into a very similar situation, agrees with me 100 percent.

I mean let's face it, any idiot can go into a program that has a huge number of players to draw from in a heavily populated area and enter into a winning a situation without completely screwing it up. However, it is truly a person of special character who will enter into a struggling program, go out and get his or her ass kicked day in and day out, and still can't wait to get to the field the next day. That's when you will know beyond the shadow of a doubt that you love the game of baseball and you love coaching.

Never during those four years at Conrad Weiser did I not want to show up at the ballpark. It was never a chore; it was never a burden. I absolutely could not wait to get to the field every day and smell that fresh cut grass and partake in the greatest game ever created.

So when I say winners have pride, that's where all success starts, with that burning desire deep inside your soul to accomplish the best. I was proud to wear my Conrad Weiser baseball hat everywhere I went while I coached there. I was proud to say that I was part of a program that was on its way up.

Several of those players have gone onto college and some have entered the work force. Most of them have been very successful in their lives thus far, and their pride motivated them to keep going out day in and day out and battling. They are all better young men for those efforts today.

So always be sure that your own personal pride is what motivates you in everything you do, on the field and off. Ultimately, pride motivated even professional baseball players. Pride that they were determined to stick out through high school, college, twelve-hour bus trips, and thousand-dollar-a-month salaries in the minors. The millions of dollars a year that they make today should be the fruit of their motivation, not the motivation itself.

I mentioned the success I had achieved in sales earlier, and that my self-pride was always my motivator. Again, this is something that I can't stress enough; love what you do and who you do it for.

Regardless of the amount of money you make, if you do not enjoy what you do, it will eventually become a chore. I had spent five very successful years selling building materials for both 84 Lumber and Wickes Lumber; I loved every minute of it. I had personal relationships with my customers and several of them are still my friends today. Unfortunately, it had become a chore. What started out as a very team-oriented environment at Wickes Lumber, quickly deteriorated. I had a boss who had no concept of what being part of team was. He felt that he was the only reason that our center was having the success that we were experiencing. Instead of building up teamwork, he looked for ways to tear it down. I was still selling hundreds of thousands of dollars worth of material a month but it was a chore. It was no fun, and it turned into a grind. I was on pace to earn over a hundred thousand dollars again the year I walked away from it. Most people thought I had gone insane to walk away from that job to start a small sporting goods business full time. That decision, although I would make it again today under the same circumstances, caused some extreme financial hardship for my wife and me, but even she would tell you that it was the correct decision. She could see the stress the situation had created and supported me. This is another extremely good example of teamwork carrying over into real life. We went through some extremely tough times because of that decision and we had to pull together as a team like we never had before to get through it and we did. Those times were extremely difficult and they were a true test of our love for each other and our teamwork. We survived and we came out of those difficult times with a stronger relationship than ever. Again though, money is only a temporary fix, if you're not happy in your career, the money will not be enough after a while.

Ultimately, just about every customer that I had left the company well within a year after I had left: the $4.5 million in sales went elsewhere. Whether or not my boss ever figured out how to be a team player, I'll never know, but it certainly should be a lesson here. He was fired a few years later and I actually ended up coming back to Wickes and with me, so did the majority of those customers. I worked for

Wickes for another two years or so. I was there while the company filed Chapter 11 bankruptcy and was eventually purchased by another company, Bradco Supply. It was an extremely difficult time to be a salesman for this company, having to assure customers that we could actually get the materials to them as our company struggled through the bankruptcy process. It turned into an extremely daunting task at times. For us to succeed, we again had to pull together as a team and we eventually did. Again though, the primary motivation at that time for us as a company was to satisfy our customers. With everything else that was going on in the company at that time with the bankruptcy process, if you were motivated solely by money, it would have made for an even more stressful situation.

C H A P T E R 4

Focus On The Positive

*I*f you're coaching baseball in this day and age, it shouldn't take long for you to figure out that the kids nowadays do not respond very well to yelling and screaming and negativity. Right, wrong, or indifferent, that's a fact.

To get the most out of your players, you need to stress the positive, not the negative. Now I'm not saying that you can never tell a kid he screwed up or that you never raise your voice on the baseball field. Every player who I have ever coached has probably heard me blow my stack once in a while, but what I am saying is that you have to "pick your spots."

To publicly undress a kid in the middle of a game is never the right approach. The game is for the players. I've always said a good coach is like a good umpire, when the game is over, the fans shouldn't even know either one was there.

Fans do not come to see coaches rant and rave at players and umpires. They are there to see the kids play the game. The sooner you understand this as a coach, the better off you will be. If you need to be the center of attention during the game, you've got some serious issues and I would strongly suggest some type of counseling.

The one thing you need to remember as a coach is that every kid is out there giving it his best shot. They are going to make mistakes, and they are kids. The best big leaguers make mistakes; it is part of the game. As a coach, you need to help keep a player to stay focused after an error. The last thing you want him to do is to carry that mistake into the dugout and into his next plate appearance.

I've always felt that the best approach with a player is to pull him aside after he makes a mistake and tell him man to man what he did wrong and what he needs to do to prevent it from happening again. You will earn his respect that way and get much quicker results than if you scream across the field at him and make him feel like crap.

I guess I like to picture myself as the strong, silent type. Very seldom will I yell at a player, and when I do, he knows he is in the doghouse.

Now don't get me wrong, I am not saying that I let the inmates run the asylum, they all know who the boss is. They also know their limits. I treat them with respect and they treat me with respect. If they push me to the edge, they know that there will be consequences.

As a coach, you need to make sure that your players understand the rules. Regardless of the level that you are coaching at, you should try to eliminate all of the gray areas. Make sure they understand what you expect of them at all times. Open lines of communication are of the utmost importance when coaching at any level.

Focusing on the positive doesn't mean that you ignore the negative. The negative must be addressed or it will fester like a cancer. You have to address the negative and then reinforce it with the positives.

If you're addressing your team after a loss, they are already down on themselves, so you do not want to stand there and berate them about the loss and focus on all of the negatives. You *must* address the negatives, but focus more on the positives.

I've never personally gotten upset over a loss if I felt that we were outplayed or beaten by a better team that day. What drives me crazy, however, is if I felt that a lesser opponent beat us because we weren't focused or ready to play.

If we lost because we made four fielding errors, I can actually live with that; it's baseball, that sort of thing will happen every once in a while. On the other hand, if we made four errors because we weren't hustling or playing hard in the first place and being just plain lazy, that is a different story. That is a mental breakdown; you would have to address it immediately.

Players need to understand that regardless of how talented they are as a team, they just can't go out on the field and go through the motions. It just doesn't work that way. Every day in practice you have to keep working hard, you have to keep working on the fundamentals, over and over and over again. You have to be continually developing that muscle memory, creating the correct habits so that after time, it just comes naturally.

When we practice indoors as an organization over the winter, we'll actually work out with kids that range in age from nine years old to eighteen years old. We keep working on the same things over and over, fundamentals of the game. I laugh sometimes because you can see that some of the older kids think that they're wasting their time sometimes— working on such basic drills.

A few years ago, I started making an annual trek to Clearwater, Florida, for Spring Training. The Philadelphia Phillies drafted one of the players that I had coached previously, Nick Evangelista, so the first trip actually came about on a whim. We were talking on the phone one night and decided that it would be cool for me to come down and visit the next weekend. So I did, my fourteen-year-old nephew and I hopped on a plane on a Friday afternoon and flew back on Sunday morning. It was great.

Nick was entering his second year of pro ball. In his first he spent the summer playing for the GCL Phillies and then got a late season call-up to Lakewood. So this spring he was hoping to move up to High Class A. Because the trip was more to hang out with Nick than to do anything else, we saw only half of a Major League Spring Training game on the Friday night that we had arrived. It was only 40 degrees that night in Clearwater, the coldest night all spring, and because of traffic in Florida as we were coming from the airport to the stadium, we got to the game late. We also left early because it was so cold.

That Saturday, we went over to the Phillies Minor League Complex in the morning and that turned out to be the best part of the trip. I sat there for three to four hours just walking from each field in the cloverleaf taking in the drills that were being done. I'd watch pitchers cover first base literally for an hour, I'd watch a drill where the coach would hit a ball to the left field gap and the centerfielder would chase it down and come up throwing to third through the cut-off man, and seeing pitcher after pitcher just run over to back up third. They kept doing it, again over and over and over. Another drill had just infielders and a pitcher, and the coach would feed balls into a pitching machine that was pointed directly into the sky to replicate towering infield pop-ups. The infielders would converge on the incoming ball while the pitcher stood there and directed traffic. Again, they just kept doing it over and over again. Repetition of the fundamentals at the professional level—what a concept! I mean simple stuff, basic stuff, covering first base, backing up third base, directing traffic on a fly ball—how much more basic could you get? It was great. I was in heaven, just soaking it all in and making mental notes.

You have to realize that you are dealing with the cream of the crop here, the best of the best and they still work on the fundamentals of the game over and over. Ground balls, fly balls, double plays, these guys will field them, catch them, and turn them two or three hundred times some days. I certainly think that if the best trained professional athletes can work on repetition of the fundamentals constantly, most of the kids in our youth programs could use some brushing up as well.

I use that story every winter when I see our sixteen-, seventeen-, and eighteen-year-olds getting apathetic during the "basic drills" that we conduct during our winter workouts. It amazes me how kids at that age start to think that they are beyond working on the fundamentals of the game. They truly believe that they have reached an age where they have mastered the basics of the game. Quite honestly, just that concept alone baffles me. That anyone, especially a child, could actually believe that he or she has mastered the game. Probably one of the things that has always drawn me to the game of baseball, is that I will never master it—not as a player, not as a coach, not as an administrator. I am always looking to learn something more about the game.

When we play another team, I observe them. I watch their pregame drills, how they conduct themselves, how they interact, everything. I watch and I observe, for two reasons. First of all, to "size them up." You can tell an awful lot about a team before you ever play them by seeing how they go about their business during their pregame routine. I can usually tell before the first pitch is even thrown what type of game we are going to be in for. The second reason I observe, is to see what I can learn from them. What can I pick up from them that I can use for my team? What is it that they did that I would want my players to do, as well as what they do that I *do not* want my players to do.

Even when I am at a professional game, I do the same thing. I watch and I take it all in. I love to get to the ballpark early so that I can watch batting practice and pregame warm-ups. I'll notice my wife looking at me oddly sometimes out of the corner of my eye. When we first started attending games together she would always ask me what's wrong and I would simply reply, "Nothing, I'm just taking it all in." Sometimes I still feel like I'm five years old again when I get there, but my amazement and observance is for different reasons now—or maybe not. Either way, my wife understands now, she won't ask me what's wrong anymore. I think she finally understands some of the things that make me tick. As I watch, I try to see what makes these guys who they are, what is it that they do that sets them apart. Sure, natural God-given talent is a huge part of it, but that's not all. Talent will get you so far, but to really get you to the top, it takes much more than just talent. There are those intangibles that separate the men from the boys. Good coaches can recognize it, but none of them can quite find the words to describe it. Some people call it heart, some people call it work ethic, and some people call it passion. I personally think that it's a combination of all of the above and more. It's something that can't be coached or taught, it's in your blood. So with all that being said, I think that I've discovered how to dispel that myth of these teenagers thinking that they have learned all there is to know about the game, I pretty much tell them that if Cole Hamels can practice covering first base a thousand times every March, so can they. It really works, they'll step it up.

Eight-five percent of what I do as a coach is something that I copied from someone else, something that I learned from somewhere else. Whether it is practice drills, pregame motivation, or just how I put my uniform on, it's almost all copied. In a way, I think that is the truest honor that you can ever give another human being, by taking something that you have learned from the person and passing it on to someone else. I can only hope that someday down the road, one of my former players who will then be coaching will gather his team around in a huddle and say to them, "I want to share something with you guys that an old coach of mine once taught me…Coach Clouser used to say…"

Now that would be my legacy.

Although I am a huge Boston Red Sox fan, I am also an associate scout for the Phillies, so I have continued to make that annual trek to Clearwater every year since then. Nick was released a few years ago, but I still go. We go to see more big league games now and we stay for longer than just three days, but I always make a point to get over to the minor league complex to watch those drills. It's like therapy for me, it just gets my blood flowing. This past year, we went to Fort Myers to see the Red Sox. We went and hung out at their minor league complex for a little while and sure enough, I learned something new there as well.

I once heard the phrase that "practice doesn't make perfect, but perfect practice makes perfect." That is so true, if you go out and field a thousand balls the wrong way, you may have practiced, but what did you really accomplish by practicing the wrong way? Now you'll have to go out and field three thousand balls the correct way before you can fix it. It is so important to emphasize that kids keep doing things the right way. The more you can drill that into them when they are younger, the easier it is for them when they are older.

CHAPTER 5

Attitude Is Everything

Attitude is everything. Now that's an original one, isn't it? There I go again with that copying thing. Anyway, there's no truer statement. As a coach, a leader, and a mentor, *your* attitude *is* everything. If you're having a lousy day, if you're arguing with your wife, if your kids just aggravated you before you left the house to come to the ballpark, you can't let that affect you. There is no way that you can allow your players to see that you do not have your "A game." Whether you're a baseball coach or a supervisor at your "day job," you are a leader. You have to rise above all of those distractions and continue to lead your players or your employees. If you can't do that, then you really are not a leader at all.

It still amazes me how a lot of youth baseball coaches really do not believe that they are role models to their players. The same goes for those professional athletes who wish to hide behind that veil by saying they're not role models as well. You think that the hundreds of thousands of kids who have their parents buy your jersey don't look up to you? Come on, what world are you living in?

Anyway, I digressed. Youth coaches are role models, whether they like it or not. Greater role models than you would ever think. A youth coach isn't only a role model to the players, but also to their parents and his peers. I once heard a coach—who I am embarrassed to say, coached in our organization—tell his players point blank, that he was not a role model to them. That they should do as he said and not as he did. He is no longer a coach in our organization. He wasn't let go for that statement alone, but because he truly believed that statement and conducted himself as such. Hindsight being twenty-twenty, we should have acted upon that statement alone, but we didn't. We won't let that happen ever again.

If I still haven't convinced you that if you are in a leadership role that you are a role model, let me go one step further.

I was invited to speak at the National Alliance of Youth Sports Annual Convention in San Antonio, Texas, a few years ago regarding wood vs. metal bats in youth sports. Just as a side note, I am on the wood bat side of that fence, but that's not the point of this story.

While at the convention, I had the opportunity to hear Emmitt Smith give his keynote address to the attendees. Yes, the same Emmitt Smith who is the NFL's leading rusher, NFL TV commentator, and Hall of Famer. Within the first few minutes of his address, he mentioned two coaches who had a great influence on his life. They were his eight-year-old and nine-year-old Pee Wee Football coaches. Not Jimmy Johnson or Galen Hall, but the first two adults who he stepped on the field with. Don't get me wrong; he spoke very highly of both Jimmy Johnson and Galen Hall as well as his speech went on, but I found it amazing that the *first* two guys that he mentioned were his first two youth football coaches. If that story alone doesn't make you understand how you influence a young person's life as a youth coach, again, you're missing the point.

Emmitt Smith achieved the highest pinnacle that he could on the grandest stage of his sport and he still remembered by names the first two football coaches he had when he was eight and nine years old. Just take a minute to think about that and tell me that you are not a role model.

Just to drive that point home more, even now in my early forties, I can still remember my first two Little League coaches, Coach Heist and

Coach Distasio, as if I had played for them yesterday. It was 1978 with the Oley Valley Youth League, the team was called the Red Sox, which is also a large part of how I became a Boston Red Sox fan, but that's another story in its own right. I was actually the youngest kid on the team. My mom, because she basically ran the concession stand and was heavily involved in the organization as a volunteer, pulled some strings to allow the organization to let me play on the team a year earlier than I was supposed to. Most of the players on the team were either nine or ten-years old, I wouldn't turn nine until July, after the season was actually over, so my mom pulled some strings and got me onto a team. We had a very good team and with me being the youngest on the team, I was just a bit intimidated as well. I was also pretty shy, but Coach Heist and Coach Distasio both made me feel as though I fit right in even though I was a year younger than everyone else on the team. Right from the start, I loved the game of baseball. I can only imagine that Coach Heist and Coach Distasio had a lot to do with that. They taught us the fundamentals and most of all, they taught us to have fun and enjoy the game. Little did I know that this would be the beginning of what has turned out to be a lifelong love affair with the game of baseball. I still can't put my finger on what draws me to this game completely—whether it's simply the timelessness of it, the symmetry, obviously the teamwork, or the way that it can help us to relate to life. I guess all of those things draw me to the game to an extent.

The game is so symbolic of life. That fact is so simple and so obvious, yet so many people miss it. As in life, there are things that you must face alone in the game; however, you always have your teammates (your family) right there with you to cheer you on and help you when you need it. As in life, you start at home and your ultimate goal is to return home, to come full circle, so to speak. There are times when you can accomplish that feat on your own, perhaps by hitting a home run, but for the vast majority of the time, as in life, you need the help of your teammates to get you back to where you started, home plate. Along the way, a teammate may have to sacrifice himself to help you get closer to home. In return, there will be times during the game (life) that you will have to sacrifice to help a teammate as well. Everything that you do affects your teammates, your family, every decision that you make, the way you go about making those decisions all have an effect on all of those around you, your teammates, your friends, your family as it relates to the game of life.

So much time and effort by so many people goes into the very simple task of returning home, getting back to where you started, and coming full circle, just like life itself.

As my first season of baseball played out, I was having a blast, our team was good, we couldn't lose, the coaches were awesome, and I was having the time of my life. There was just this one little flaw in my game at this point; I was scared to death to swing the bat. I mean literally by the midway point of our season, probably seven or eight games in, I had literally yet to swing the bat. It wasn't because I didn't play; it was Little League, everyone played. I simply just never swung the bat. I would go to the plate, and either strike out looking or walk. Again, we were young kids, so the chances of seeing four balls before seeing three strikes in a plate appearance were literally about 50/50. Obviously, I couldn't tell you my exact stats, but at this point, I probably did reach base about half of the time that I came to the plate. I remember running the bases quite a bit. I really enjoyed that part of the game, but for whatever reason, I was just scared to death to swing the bat in a game. In practice, I loved hitting, in the game, I was terrified—can't tell you why, but I was.

So here we were, halfway through our season, and I still hadn't taken the bat off my shoulders and something happened that I will never forget. As my turn to bat came up, we had the bases loaded and Coach Distasio walked over to me, bent down, put his arm around me, and gently said, "Danny, you do know, son, that you can't ever get a hit if you don't swing the bat." Pretty simple advice, yet as I look back on it now, was much more profound today than what it was to my eight-year-old ears at the time.

So with Coach Distastio's advice fresh in my mind I stepped to the plate determined that no matter what, I was going to swing the bat at the first pitch that I saw. I did, and I ended up smoking a base-clearing double down the right field line. I was flying high, as I stood on second base; I looked into the bench area and saw my teammates' excitement that we had just scored three runs. Then I made eye contact with Coach Distasio and he simply gave me a little smile and a thumbs-up. I'd like to say that I waited on the pitch and that it was outside and that I used perfect form to go the other way with it and drive it down the right field line, but that wasn't that case. I was swinging no matter what. That pitch could have been over my head or in the dirt and I was going to swing at it. I had made my mind up as I walked to the plate after Coach Distasio talked to me. I just happened to be late with my swing and the ball went down the right field line, but that didn't matter to me or anyone else at that point.

I couldn't honestly tell you if I had another hit for the remainder of that season, but that first one I will never forget. From that point on, I wasn't afraid to swing the bat anymore. In fact, my young philosophy on hitting changed quite drastically, I went from the never swing the bat philosophy, to the swing at just about everything philosophy, changing from playing it safe to willing to take a chance. I also carried that philosophy into life.

As I said before, I'm sure at the time that both Coach Distasio and I never realized what effect that one simple sentence, "Danny, you do know, son, that you can't ever get a hit if you don't swing the bat," would have on my life. As my life has gone on, I have heard Coach Distasio say that same thing to me many, many times. Whenever there had come a time in my life where a difficult decision had to be made, I would often hear the words of my first Little League coach on that wonderful spring day saying to me, "Danny, you do know, son, that you can't ever get a hit if you don't swing the bat."

So in most cases, I decided to take the chance and swing the bat. Metaphorically, that's what I hear Coach Distasio saying now when I replay in my mind, "You have to take a chance, you have to swing that bat, you can't be afraid to fail and if you do fail, who cares, you'll get another chance to swing the bat again."

Again, I'm sure that at the time, Coach Distasio had no idea that that little bit of simple, yet so obvious advice would have such an effect on my entire life, but it did. He was just trying to get an eight-year-old kid to overcome his fear of batting in a game; however, it was probably his approach that made it so effective. That was really the key, the combination of what he said and how he said it is what left an indelible mark on my life that day. He could have shouted the same thing to me from the coach's box and I don't think that it would have had the same effect on me. Although he may not have meant for it to embarrass me, it more than likely would have. He took the time to walk up to me, meet me at my level by bending down to speak to me, put his arm around me, and look me in the eye. That was the key, the approach as much as the advice is what made the difference. He knew the right combination of what to say and how to say it to get through to me. Had he walked up to me and told me to stop being such a wimp and swing the bat for once, more than likely, it wouldn't have had the same effect on me.

That is one thing that we must always remember as coaches, that we are teachers, that we are role models, and that we have an incredible effect on a young person's life. Everything you say is heard, and you never know when you say something to a player whether or not he will latch on to it and keep it with him for his entire life.

I hadn't seen Coach Distasio for many years, but he left a lasting mark on my life. Shortly after that first season, my mother and father got divorced and I moved to Florida with my mom. I returned to Oley each summer, but spent most of the time at my grandparents' house in Birdsboro because my Dad drove a truck and was away during the week. I saw a few friends that lived close to us and who were within bike riding distance, but for the most part I didn't really get a chance to see most of my friends from those first Little League days.

When I moved back to Pennsylvania in 1983, entering ninth grade, I returned to Oley excited about the prospect of seeing my old friends and most of all getting to play baseball at Oley and learning from one of the true masters of the game, Coach Bob Rentschler. I had known Coach Rentschler for years. He had coached my brother when I was playing Little League at the Youth League and was one of those individuals that you were simply drawn to. He had that charisma about him that just knocked your socks off. He was the type of guy that would go out of his way to make you feel special. My first day back at Oley, I had Coach Rentschler for gym class and he immediately remembered who I was. That, to this day impressed me. I mean I was gone for four and half years. My brother, who was my connection to Coach Rentschler, had graduated from Oley five years earlier and immediately enlisted in the army so it wasn't like he was still living locally to keep me fresh in his mind, so for him to remember me was very impressive in my mind.

We immediately talked about the prospect of the high school baseball season and how excited I was to be a part of it. I was only a freshman, so I would certainly be on the JV team and probably not have much of an impact there either. As I said before, I was an average player and had to work really hard just to get onto the field, but Coach Rentschler genuinely made me feel like I was part of the program, and we were only in September—the season was still another six months away. That was another characteristic of Coach Rentschler that I truly admired. Here I was, an average freshman player six months prior to the season starting, and here he was, already a legendary high school baseball coach running a very successful program. He genuinely made me feel as though I was an important part of that program, and I had never even put on an Oley Valley High School uniform yet.

As it turned out, I never did get to put on an Oley Valley High School uniform, in November of my freshman year, right at Thanksgiving, my father and I moved to the Schuylkill Valley School District and my aspirations of playing for the legendary Bob Rentschler ended abruptly.

Oley went on to win their first state championship that season in 1984. I was playing junior high baseball at Schuylkill Valley because they didn't allow freshman to try out for the high school team. It was kind of frustrating reading about Oley's success in the paper, even knowing that as a freshman, I wouldn't have actually played varsity at Oley. But I would have been part of something special and Coach Rentschler would have made sure that we all felt like we had contributed to the program's success in some small way.

Oley went on to win the state championship again in 1985 and every time that we played them, I gained a little more respect for Coach Rentschler, not because of how good his teams were, but because after every game that we played them, Coach Rentschler would come up to me and ask me how I was doing. He would ask about my family and me, and he was genuinely interested in the answers. This wasn't lip service, he had nothing to gain, he would actually have his team wait for his post-game talk with them as he and I chatted after our teams shook hands in the lines. That always meant a lot to me and still does, even today. He was a man who I never played a game for, who I had for one quarter as a high school gym teacher, who truly made a lasting impression on my life. It's because of Coach Rentschler that I personally go out of my way to learn the names of the players that are in our organization. When we have our group workouts, I make every effort to learn their names and make them understand that they are all a special part of the Berkshire Baseball program.

As an organization, we never put players' names on the back of their jerseys. We don't do it for several reasons. First, I feel that it promotes individualism; second, I want them to all understand that the name on the back of the shirt is not important—it's the name on the front of the shirt that *is* important. Lastly, by not doing it, I can't use it as a crutch. I want to know all of the players' names in our organization, not because I can read them off the back of their shirts, but because I genuinely want to know who they are and make them understand that they are all important parts of what makes Berkshire Baseball successful.

Coach Rentschler passed away at only sixty-eight years old in February of 2010; his legacy with me is that he taught me the importance of knowing people by name and genuinely making them feel like they are an important part of your program. His complete legacy is much broader, he touched thousands of young lives and many of those players are now coaching as I am. Although he is gone, his teachings will be passed on forever through those of us he touched.

Another amazing example of how baseball takes us full circle and how life many times does as well is that after not seeing Coach Distasio after over thirty years, his grandson, Nick, came to play for our organization in 2009. How ironic is it that after all of those years, we came full circle. The coach who taught me that you needed to take chances in life in order to be successful would now have his grandson playing in the very organization that might not even be around today if it wasn't for Barry Distasio telling me that it's OK to fail.

I was only twenty years old when I started the Berkshire Baseball Club and the Spring-Lawn Optimist Baseball League, I had a lot of people tell me that there was no way that I would get either of them off of the ground, mainly because of my young age, but also because it was a pretty daunting task. However, each time someone else would tell me that this couldn't be done, I'd play back that spring day in 1978 in my mind when Coach Distasio pulled me aside and gave me that simple, yet profound advice: "Danny, you do know, son, that you can't ever get a hit if you don't swing the bat."

So again, I swung the bat and with twenty-two years under our belt so far, I'd say the result was pretty much the same as that bases-clearing double down the right field line.

At our uniform handout one year, Coach Distasio's son, my former Little League teammate, Mike, and I were talking and the subject of my being a Red Sox fan came up, how the organization started out as the Berkshire Red Sox, and other small talk about our Little League days. I said to Mike that this whole thing, this Berkshire Baseball thing was pretty much his father's fault. That first team was called the Red Sox, his dad coached it, his dad taught me to take chances, and because of that, I was willing to look failure in the eye and did what everyone else was telling me couldn't be done.

We truly did come full circle, but the best part is that we're not even done yet.

So as a role model, your attitude *is* everything. A deodorant commercial back in the 1970s and '80s used the tag line, "Never let them see you sweat." That is so true as a coach and a leader. Stay calm. Stay cool. Your players will feed off you and your positive energy; they will also feed off your negative energy. Regardless of the situation, you have to keep your emotions in check. Whether you're up by ten or down by ten, you have to keep cool and stay in control.

The best managers in the world are the ones that can take all of the pressure off their players and carry it on their own shoulders without ever missing a beat or letting their players know what kind of pressure is on regarding their performance. At the college and professional ranks, an enormous amount of pressure is put on a manager to win. The most successful managers are the ones who create a buffer between those above them and their players. They're the ones who can handle all of the pressure and yet not let their players feel any of it.

Learning how to motivate your team to perform at their highest level or sometimes even higher is a difficult task to master. It is a constant juggling act between pushing them to succeed, and not pushing them over the edge. My proudest moments as a coach are not when I had the best and most talented team at my disposal, but when I had a team of underdogs and misfits who had a ton of heart. Going out and beating a team that you're better than is not hard. Going out and beating a team that is far above you, is extremely rewarding. It's truly the fruit of your labor when you see your players work as a team to achieve their common goal.

When you look at some of the best managers in the professional ranks today, you'll see the guys who can control their emotions, guys who can keep a positive twist on everything that happens. Terry Francona was one of the best at that. I'm not just saying that because he was the Boston Red Sox manager and I'm a Boston Red Sox fan. The guy truly is a class act. When I watch a major league press conference after a game on TV, I listen intently to what the manager says during that press conference. I guess I watch it a bit differently than most people, but I observe and listen just as I do to a pregame routine. Listen to see what I can learn. What are they saying in the press conference that is gaining or losing respect for their players? Francona was truly one of the best at that, he always supported his players and stayed positive regardless of the situation.

Obviously as a Red Sox fan, I have always hated the Yankees, but another guy that I've always admired, even when he wore the pinstripes, was Joe Torre. If you ever saw a camera shot of him in the dugout, you never could guess if they were winning or losing, tight game or a blowout. I was glad to see him leave New York.

Coaching in the youth ranks is no different. You have to keep your emotions in check, your players need to know that you are behind them, you have to stay positive, and you have to earn their respect. That's right, respect is earned, whether it's from a six-year-old-kid, a multimillion-dollar professional athlete, or any age in between, they won't respect you just because of the title below your name, you have to earn it. The only way to earn respect is to lead by example. Your actions have to speak louder than your words. You can't preach punctuality to your players and then show up ten minutes late every day. You can't preach teamwork and show them that you are selfish. You can't preach dedication and then miss three games during the season yourself or complain that you have to be there in the first place.

One of my proudest moments as a coach was in October of 2005. That Friday, my employer informed me that they were letting me go. My 16-U team had a tournament that weekend, our first game was less than four hours after I was just informed that I no longer had a job. Now that's some bad news. To lose your mother and your job in the same year was tough to deal with. How would I be able to stay positive this weekend? The team had underachieved all season; we were loaded with talent but never quite seemed to fire on all cylinders. We hovered around .500 all season long, it was like we would get right to the cusp of winning a tournament and come up short every time. I had called my assistant coach prior to getting to the field to tell him what had happened earlier in the day, I didn't want to risk one of the kids hearing me tell him while we were at the field, so I wanted to make sure that I told him in private. I'm still not really sure how I did it, but when I got to the field, I just put everything behind me. As I had said earlier in the book, going to the ballpark has always been very therapeutic for me and this weekend was certainly no different; it may have actually been more therapeutic than usual.

The team came out of the gates firing; we finally seemed to start clicking. We got clutch hits, great pitching performances, and very solid defense. We ended up winning our first and only tournament that season and the feeling was great. I didn't do anything special that weekend, the kids played the games, the kids rose to the occasion, I just happened to be there. But maybe, it was just the fact that I *didn't* do anything special, that had actually helped them to perform. I didn't express to them that I was in a lousy mood because I had just lost my job. I didn't tell them before our first game that I had lost my job and it would be great for them to finally go out and play the game the way that I knew they could so that they could make me feel better at the end of the weekend. I just went about the weekend with the attitude of business as usual. There was no way that I could let them see that I was torn up inside regarding the obvious uncertainty of my personal plight. I had to make sure, for them, that they had no idea what was going on. Again, I didn't do anything to win that tournament that weekend, but I certainly could have done things that would have added pressure to them and caused them to not perform to their ability.

Sometimes the toughest thing to do as a coach is to just stay out of the way and let the players play the game. There have been times when I felt that we won a game or two because I "out-coached" the other guy, but I will guarantee that there have been several more games that I can take the responsibility for the loss than the ones that I can take credit for the win. Most of the time, the kids win and lose the game, not the coach. Coaches need to understand that. As I said before, a good coach is like a good umpire, at the end of the game no one should have realized that either one was even there.

I can't stand those coaches who love to stand in the third base coaching box with a stopwatch hanging out of their pocket and barking out a batting lesson to their player while he is trying to concentrate on hitting the baseball. I think to myself, "Don't these guys realize that that's what practice is for?" I mean if you need to shout out how to hit a first pitch fastball during the game, then what the hell were you doing at practice? If your players don't know how to hit a baseball by the time the game starts, then you failed at your job. The game is for the kids to go out and play. It's not your venue as a coach to let all of the parents and fans know how much you know about hitting or fielding or pitching. They are not there to see you coach and rant and rave about how much you know about the game; they're there to watch their kid play a baseball game and see how you have taught them the skills of the game during your practices, not during the game.

That's what practice time is for, for the coach to teach. You can rant and rave all you want during practice if that's your style, that's *your* time. The game is the players' time, stay out of their way and let them play the game. If you did your job in practice, you should be able sit back and enjoy the fruits of your labor. If you realized that you missed teaching them something by watching what happens during the course of the game, make a note of it and make sure you teach them at the next practice or point it out during your post-game meeting, or better yet, do both. Just don't rant and rave and think that the third base coaching box is your personal pulpit and everyone is there to hear your baseball sermon, because they are not. They are there to watch their kids play and you shouting and drawing attention to yourself only annoys everyone around you and makes them realize that you're probably really just trying to hide some other personal shortcoming.

I just recently had a conversation with one of my players from that same 16-U team that performed so well that weekend that I lost my job. He is now twenty-three years old, a board member, and he helps the organization whenever he can. He played on our college summer team for a few years and he often helps at our workouts by coming and throwing batting practice or helping with anything else that we ask him to do. He just starting coaching with me a few seasons ago and did a fantastic job as our 16-U pitching coach. We were talking about attitude and how another coach of his would always make it very well known to his team that while he was out coaching, his wife was pissed at him for being there, his son cried when he left the house, and he often had to use personal vacation time to go on baseball trips. He was telling me how the coach always made it sound like it was a chore for him to be at a practice, game, or winter workout. He said that the coach always wanted to make sure that the players knew how much *he* was sacrificing to coach them; the players really had no idea how to react to his comments. They didn't know if the coach hated them because he had to be there or what.

At that point, I asked him about that tournament weekend that we won when he was sixteen years old, and I asked him if he knew that I had lost my job that weekend. He had no idea. That moment over six years later was the first time he heard what I was going through that weekend. I had only told him then to help emphasize the point that as a leader and a coach you can't let those around you know what's bothering you. You have to be the buffer; you have to be able to handle the pressure. You have to be able to put all of your personal problems aside when you get around the team. These guys are kids; they have their own problems to deal with as teenagers. They should feel comfortable knowing that they can come to you with *their* problems, whether it's a baseball-related problem or if their girlfriend just dumped them. You're an adult; they should be looking to you for guidance, not made to feel as if they approach you, they're just going to be another burden for you to deal with on top of your wife that hates you and your crying son.

That's something that I just can't grasp, how a coach can stand in front of his players and their parents complaining about having to be at the baseball field so early in the morning or anything else for that matter. Again, how can you preach to your players about attitude when yours is so bad? Attitude is always a reflection of leadership and that will never change. If you don't like your team's attitude, you probably want to take a look in the mirror. Change normally has to start from the top. If it's really a chore for you to be at the baseball field, then you shouldn't be coaching. You're doing your players and their parents a grave disservice. It goes back to what I said earlier in the book: love what you do and who you do it for. If you can't honestly say that you love what you do and who you do it for, you need to make a change.

CHAPTER 6

A Quality Called Commitment

*A*s I said once before, the best stuff that I have taught to someone else, I learned from somebody else. I do have a few original ideas and theories, but honestly, the best ones are the ones that I have gotten from someone else.

A few years back, I was interviewing for a job and the company did this very in-depth online interview. At the end of the interview, they sent you to a link that had a copy of an article from the *Saturday Evening Post*, written by Art Williams. The article was titled "A Quality Called Commitment." I was offered the job, but didn't take it largely because of what I read in that article. I really thought that position was a great opportunity and it certainly offered some ways to make a nice income; however, the truth was that deep down inside, I knew that I could not make the proper commitment to this company to do the job right in order for both us to be successful.

To this day, it is still one of the best articles that I have ever read. I kept a copy of it, refer to it often, and at the beginning of each baseball season, I give a copy of it to my players in hopes that they "get it."

For me to write a book that has a chapter that refers to commitment without sharing this article would be a grave injustice. I hope that you can get as much out of it as I have over the years...

A QUALITY CALLED COMMITMENT

In a popular song of the '50's, they called that special quality "heart." I call it "commitment." Whatever you name it, the old song is right – "you gotta have it" if you want to make it in any area of life.

Commitment – it's a big word full of big promises for those who take it seriously. It's just a quality, something you can't see or feel. But it's a fact of life: All goals, dreams, ideas and hopes in this world fade away without this vital ingredient. Look at any story of success and accomplishment, and commitment is one element turning up again and again. There are many roads to success and happiness, but none will get you there if you don't take commitment along as your walking stick.

Many people today are not willing to make a total commitment to anything. It's not because they're irresponsible; rather, they've been hurt disappointed or discouraged by the sometimes painful, frustrating experiences they've encountered in life. Some have failed in business or in their personal lives and chosen to take the safe route so they won't get hurt again. I've observed in my working life that a sure step on the road to failure – often the fatal step – is loss of ability to make a commitment.

Too many people do just enough to get by. For uncommitted people, the day-to-day frustrations of life seem monumental because they're not viewed as part of the big picture, one step toward a long-range goal.

Lack of commitment causes many people's business failures. It's not lack of skills or lack of talent. Sometimes it's not even lack of energy. Some people work and work but just seem to spin their wheels. Often the vital missing ingredient is total commitment.

Several years ago I hired a very capable woman as a sales representative for my company. A college professor, she wanted the increased earning potential and opportunity of a sales career.

Ten months later, she came to me exhausted and totally discouraged. She was working furiously, making calls, seeing clients – but getting nowhere. At first I couldn't see what her problem was. Obviously active and smart, she was making an impressive effort.

And then she told me her concerns. Because she had taken a one-year leave of absence from the college, she had only two more months to decide whether she could make it in the sales business; she would lose her tenure and all her benefits from the college if she didn't return.

That was her problem: She hadn't made a total commitment to her new work, and it was showing. In the back of her mind, she knew she could return to her teaching job if things didn't work out in her new career. She thought she was holding a trump card, but her trump card was holding her – holding her back from making a total commitment to the new job.

I advised her that it was time to make a choice. If she really wanted to make it in sales, she had to go out on a limb. She couldn't have another choice – something "held back" just in case. She had to make the decision to give up her tenure at the college and to give up any thought of returning to her former job.

Not only did she make this decision, but, as a final measure of commitment, she packed up her family and moved to another city to open new sales territory. The change in her outlook was soon apparent. Three months after the move, her income for one month was greater than she had earned annually at the college. In another three months, she was promoted to an executive position within the company.

In present-day society, it seems that people want things to come without any effort. I find many people looking for the perfect job – one without too much work or too many headaches. Well, folks, that's not life. If you want big rewards, you've got to pay a price. There are sacrifices, and sometimes the going gets tough. But 99 percent of the things people worry about never happen. If you don't counteract your fears, worry can defeat all your initial enthusiasm and positive feelings.

To succeed, the effort to counteract those fears can and must be made. Total commitment to a goal or a dream will make bearable the frustrations and disappointments of any undertaking. Without commitment, the things that are possible, but tough, become impossible.

This is true both in business and in personal life. Marriage is good example; like business, it requires a total commitment to succeed. Every person does things that irritate other people. All sorts of disagreements and outright arguments crop up. Each person has some traits or habits that the other person doesn't like. Commitment to a person, however, changes the focus from the annoying incidents to the positive, happy incidents. It's a matter of seeing the beauty of the rose, without noticing its thorns.

Committed people see things around them in a special way. They're just all-around different, and that difference makes them stand out above the crowd.

Committed people are loyal. They have their priorities in order. They don't switch from one thing to another or do something halfway. Most important, others know they can count on them. They know the "committers" will be there in good times and bad. Both friends and associates know they're in the game until the final whistle.

Committed people are dreamers. They base their futures on something they can't see — namely, their faith in, the goals they've set for, themselves.

Committed people are often controversial. Because they are working toward something they believe in with all their hearts and minds, they're not bound by "what other people think," and they're not afraid of the disapproval or disagreement of the masses. They know that they're doing what is right for them, and they have inner peace from committing themselves fully to such a decision.

Commitment brings out a special toughness. Committed people don't quit. Commitment brings out a special endurance. If you're committed to a good cause or effort, and you know you're going to make it work, something amazing happens. Suddenly you have more energy, both physically and mentally. (Mental confusion and conflict, not a heavy work load, drains energy.) Suddenly, you have incredible endurance and a positive, excited outlook. Committed people blur the line between work and play. They love their work and they want to do more and more, not less. Work becomes a pleasure and a challenge, even with its problems.

Commitment is habit forming, a way of life. Most committed people reach their goals and don't even realize it. By that time, they've upgraded their goals to even bigger ones and they're off and running.

Probably most important, committed people have something to live for. People everywhere are dying to "be happy." Committed people really are happy. They have some direction in life. They've made a commitment to something they believe in.

Compare commitment to religious belief. For many people, inner peace seems always out of reach. Only when they make a commitment to their religion can they find the peace they've been seeking.

Everything else falls into place when people find something worth committing themselves to. They can do almost anything; they can pay any price.

It sounds simple, but in truth it's not easy. Sometimes it means burning bridges, leaving something familiar behind to leap into something unknown. Yet this is why commitment is of such importance. Without it, the fears and apprehensions about changing lifestyles or careers would be too overwhelming. That one quality can make all the difference.

There are two kinds of qualities — outside and inside. Outside qualities you can obtain through learning. Inside qualities you must develop from experience and such living, intangible things as faith and hope. Commitment is an inside quality. You may have to look inside for it, but it's there when you're ready to make the decision and devote your closest attention and best efforts to it.

The line between failure and success is so fine, we're often on the line and don't even know it. It's important to realize that our "inside" qualities — or lack of them — can be responsible for the way we go.

You can't see commitment. You can only see results. But then, what difference does it make? When you have it, you'll know it's there. So will everyone else.

~ Art Williams

Reprinted with permission from the Saturday Evening Post Society, a division of BFL&MS, Inc 1983

One thing that I am truly grateful for is that I have over time figured out the ability to know when to say yes and I know when to say no. It wasn't always like that way for me; in fact, I pissed a lot of people off in the past by saying yes to something or someone that I should have said no to.

If you cannot make a commitment to something, you are much better off by just saying no upfront as opposed to saying yes and then pissing people off because you didn't follow through.

I had a client like that once. This guy always wanted to be everybody's best friend. He wanted to be the man in the middle of everything. He was notorious for committing to something and then not following through with it. It didn't even matter what he was committing to, he would just say yes to everyone about everything and then instead of following through with what he had committed to, he would try to figure out how to get out of it afterward.

This happened with everything, whether it was accepting a job that his company had no business even attempting, making a commitment to donate money to an organization, it didn't matter, he always said yes— whether he meant it or not.

In his mind, and what he would tell his employees, was that it was good customer service to always give the customer what they want, even if you don't know how to do it. I never understood his philosophy because in his failure to follow through with commitments, he lost more customers than he ever would have if he had just been upfront with them and let them know that he couldn't handle it in the first place.

I've always been a firm believer in the under-promise and over-deliver theory. If you think that you can get something done in three days, and then tell the customer that it will take four days. When you show up on the third day with the completed project, your customer is ecstatic because you got it done a day early. On the other hand, go ahead and deliver it a day late and you may have very well have lost the customer. Life is filled with enough obstacles and things that can naturally go wrong that there is absolutely no point in creating additional obstacles for yourself.

So whether in the business world or baseball, you have to be committed. Coaches have to be committed if they are going to get their players to be committed. I often refer to the bacon and egg breakfast when I am telling people about commitment. In a bacon and egg breakfast, you have two animals that took part in making that breakfast happen, a pig and a chicken. The chicken was involved in making that breakfast take place; the pig was committed to making that breakfast take place. When I am out recruiting players, I am looking for the pigs. I want guys that eat, sleep, drink, and breathe baseball. I want guys who if we have one game a day, they're pissed because they want to play two, if we have two games a day, they want to play three. Coaches that don't have that desire will have a hard time finding players with that desire. You lead by example. If you don't want to be there, your players will not want to be there either. Everything has to come from the top.

If you coach half-assed, your players will perform half-assed.

One thing that I could never grasp in life was how somebody could just go out and do something half-assed and not think twice about it. When you think of people who work for an hourly rate and then they don't do the job right—that just baffles me. If they are at their job for eight hours a day anyway, why wouldn't they just do their job the right way? That just doesn't make sense to me.

That's a thing that I stress to my players every day at practice, I tell them we're here for two to three hours no matter what, so we might as well do what we're here to do the correct way and everyone's life will be much easier.

As I mentioned in the beginning of this book, I had actually started this project in 2003 and pretty much just dabbled with it when I could. I really wasn't committed to completing it. I wanted to complete it. I always thought about how cool it would be to complete it, but I can't honestly say that I was totally committed to completing the book. That was until November of 2008 when I received an e-mail from Jeff Potter telling me that he had just completed his book, *Whatever Happened to Baseball?* I immediately thought to myself, wow, here was a regular guy just like me and he wrote a book.

Why haven't I completed mine yet?

In Jeff's e-mail he offered to send me a copy of the book, so I responded to him and told him that I would like to read the book. At this point, I truly had no idea who Jeff Potter even was or how he even got my e-mail address. True to his word, the book arrived a few days later. Now one thing that you have to understand about me is that I enjoy reading; however, I am the type of person who will read a few chapters of a book, put it down for weeks on end and then read another few chapters. It can literally take me up to a year to read a book sometimes.

There are five books to date that I have read in my life that I literally couldn't put down once I started them. They were *Marley & Me; Tug McGraw, Ya Gotta Believe; The Last Lecture; Tuesdays with Morrie;* and *What Ever Happened to Baseball.* I don't know what it was about Jeff's book, the honesty, the way I could relate to my childhood, my coaching philosophies, I'm not totally sure, nonetheless, once I started reading the book, I couldn't put it down. It was a great book. When I completed the book, I e-mailed Jeff and we began dialogue about the book and about baseball in general.

We spoke a few times and agreed that we should get together at some point and just talk baseball. As we continued to exchange e-mails and telephone calls, our annual banquet was also approaching. During one of our conversations about a week prior to our banquet, I mentioned to Jeff that he should come and speak a little at our banquet about his book. He lived just south of Baltimore, which is only about two and a half hours away from us, so it seemed like we might be able to pull this off. Jeff agreed to speak at our banquet in between our other two speakers for the evening, Bob Soloman, promoter of a great children's book that was titled *A Glove of Their Own* (another book that I read straight through, but it was a children's book, so I'm not sure that you can count that), and former big leaguer Ozzie Virgil. At the banquet, Jeff and I spoke quite a bit about baseball and about me writing my book as well. We got together again a few more times over the next couple of weeks, I gave him a copy of my manuscript, and continued to pick his brain on how to go about getting my book published.

One day, as we were meeting for lunch just north of Baltimore, Maryland, Jeff said to me, "Dan, if you're really going to go through with this, you need to start telling everyone you know that you're writing a book."

"What do you mean?" I replied, "...and why should I do that?"

Jeff just kind of chuckled and said, "The fear of failure."

I just kind of stared at him blankly for a minute or two, and then he said, "Right now you have no commitment to this project. You have nothing to lose. If you stop writing today, no one other than your wife and I will even know that you never completed a project that meant a lot to you.

"If you start telling people what you're doing, you're now exposing yourself to the possible embarrassment of not completing it. If you tell them you're writing a book, they are going to ask you how far you are. They are going to push you to succeed because you seem like the type of person to me who genuinely wants to not let people down.

"In your mind, you're now going to pressure yourself to make sure it gets done. Your fear of failure will make you commit to getting this done.

"If you're serious, start telling people what you're doing, then you're committed and you'll get it done."

I again just sat there and thought about what he had just said to me. As much as I wanted to reach across the table and choke him, I couldn't, because I knew that he was 100 percent right.

If I was going to continue to half-ass this, I should just stop, but if I was going to do it, I had to commit to it. He was right. I had to start telling people what I was doing. His theory of the fear of failure was right on the money. If I told people what I was doing, the last thing that I would want to do is make them think that I didn't finish what I had started.

From that day on, I made the commitment to get this completed. I had lunch with several friends, told them what I was doing, gave them some copies of what I had written up to that point, and made a conscious effort to sit down and type whenever I could. I set a deadline for myself, missed it, set another one, and nailed it.

I was now committed. I was determined to get it done. Jeff Potter challenged me that day. Jeff Potter forced me to let go of my inhibitions and drop my defenses by exposing myself to people I knew and therefore pushing me to make a commitment. If it wasn't for lunch that day with Jeff Potter, the release date of this book may not have been until 2020 or maybe even never.

It still took me another few years after that lunch meeting to get it done, but I was committed. I told people and people would ask me how it was going when I saw them. That pushed me to get it wrapped up and completed.

A few years ago, in 2006 our Berkshire Red Sox 18-U team started the season slowly. I had coached these kids during the previous two years on my 16-U team, and they had seriously underachieved. They had moved up to a different coach this year, but seemed like they were headed for another disappointing and underachieving season. What you have to understand is that our 18-U Showcase team is by far the bench-mark program of our organization, if this team doesn't win thirty games in a season, many consider it a down year.

Well these guys were sitting at 19-13-1 heading into their final two tournaments of the year; they hadn't won a tournament championship all year and a thirty win season was obviously not going to happen.

Somehow, someway, these kids finally "got it." I don't honestly know what happened. I don't know if they remembered something that we had said to them in the previous two seasons or if something Randy Strausser, their current coach, had said to them, or if they finally just realized that they wanted to be remembered in the organization for something positive as opposed to being a team that underachieved.

Our entire organization had arrived at the dorms at the *Sports at the Beach* facility in Rehoboth Beach, Delaware, on Friday night, and on Saturday morning, the majority of our 18-U Showcase team showed up

at the field with Mohawk haircuts— they were determined to finish the season on their terms. The new hair-cuts brought on a new attitude as well; the team adopted the saying, "If we're going to be here, we might as well win!" Basically taking to task that they were no longer going to half-ass it, they were going to play to their ability and they were mak-ing a commitment to each other that they'd give 110 percent the rest of the way.

They held true to their word, went 4-0-1 that weekend, and picked up their first tournament championship of the season. Still sitting on a 23-13-2 record heading into their final weekend, thirty wins seemed out of reach. Especially considering they were finishing the season by having to travel almost three thousand miles to compete in the 132 team Las Vegas Baseball Academy Desert Fall Classic. Obviously, for this group, the only team in the event from east of the Mississippi, to go out and win this nationally renowned tournament was never going to happen.

However, these cardiac kids had other plans. They weren't traveling almost three thousand miles to visit the strip, which UNLV head coach, Buddy Gouldsmith had reiterated to them during our visit to his campus prior to the tournament starting. They had determined that they were there to win a tournament and win a tournament they did. They went 7-0 against the toughest competition that they had faced all year long. They came from behind in six of the seven games that they ended up playing in that weekend and on Sunday, as if having to win three games wasn't enough, they went ten innings in both their quarter-final game and the Championship Game to win the whole thing. They went 11-0-1 in their final twelve games and finished with a mark of 30-13-2 on the season, the fifth year in a row that our Red Sox 18-U team had recorded thirty wins. This group of kids from small-town Berks County, Pennsylvania, played with the big boys from the West Coast and came out on top. They proved that once they committed themselves, they could do some special things on a baseball field. In a matter of two weeks, they went from going down into Berkshire Baseball history as the most talented, yet underachieving group to go through our program to a team that people will remember for winning arguably the biggest tournament that the organization has ever participated in against some incredibly talented baseball teams, simply because they made a commitment.

Although when the final pitch was thrown I was in stands and not the dugout, I still felt extremely proud of what these young men had accomplished, hoping that in a little way I may have contributed to their success by something that I had taught them during their previous two seasons.

Being a coach is a lot like being a parent in some respects. The way our organization is structured, our coaching staff gets to spend at the most two years with any one group of kids. It's amazing how close you can get to a group of young men during that time period, and then sometimes it seems like just as they are about to harvest their fruit,

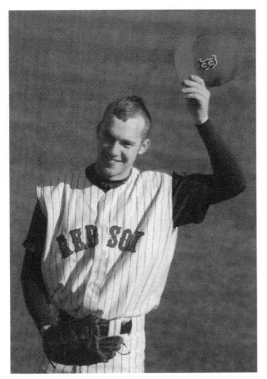

you send them to the next level. Every time that happens, I think to myself, just once, I would like to move up with these guys and be the guy who reaps the benefits. Then I again think about what my mother taught me about parenthood. As I said once before, she told me that as a parent, God requires me to teach my children two things in life, the first is to teach them how to walk and the second is to teach them how to walk away. I agree with her more and more every day that the second requirement is a whole lot tougher than the first. As a coach, you have to learn how to do the same thing. You're only going to be able to be with them for so long and at some point they are going to move on and play for someone else. Your only goal as a coach should be to make sure that you give them something of substance that they can use throughout the rest of their careers and more importantly, their lives.

I also like to refer to commitment as loyalty. Throughout my life, I have been loyal, almost to a fault. I've rooted for the same baseball team my entire life, through good and bad. Football, basketball, and hockey, the same thing, I've rooted for the same teams my entire life. I've never been the type of person to change teams, once I make a decision, I stick with it. For better or for worse, I am very much a creature of habit. I've used pretty much the same infield/outfield routine for almost all twenty-two years that I've coached; I've used the same signs for almost my entire coaching career as well. One can ask what that has to do with loyalty and commitment. The answer is somewhat simple in that those traits can pretty much carry over to loyalty and commitment.

As I mentioned earlier, my one cousin told me that just about every memory she has of me involves me wearing a baseball uniform. That to me is something that I am very proud of. I believe the longevity and commitment that I have made to the Berkshire Baseball Club speaks volumes as to what is important to me as a person.

One of my biggest issues with professional baseball these days is the business side of the game, the free agency, the lack of loyalty and commitment from both players and management. I have a hard time dealing with that part of the game. I'm a firm believer that there are certain intangibles that should mean more than money. Now don't get me wrong; I'm not saying that you never change anything and I really do understand the business side of professional baseball, but I still believe that some things should be able to trump the business side of the game and players and management should be able to figure out how to do what is right.

When Dustin Pedroia signed his extension with the Boston Red Sox and obviously left several million dollars on the table, he said, "What can't I do with $40 million that I could do with $100 million? At some point, you have to stop and say, 'Listen, I'm a regular human being.' Do I need a Bentley? Absolutely not. I don't care about those kinds of things. But does this set my family and my kids up forever? Absolutely." That statement says a lot about his character, too many players nowadays are jumping on the money with no regard to anything else. It's always refreshing when you see some of them that care more than just about the money.

When the Boston Red Sox released Dwight Evans and he went to play his final season in Baltimore, I felt that that was as close to a criminal act as you could have in Major League Baseball. There are just some instances where the game should be bigger than the business. For Derek Jeter or Mariano Rivera to wear anything other than Yankee pinstripes would be equally as criminal. Just imagine if Cal Ripken Jr. had finished his career wearing anything other than an Orioles uniform; it just wouldn't have felt right. At some point, you just have to ignore the business aspect and do what is right.

I have a friend who is a young coach and it seems like just about every off-season he calls me or e-mails me to ask me to write him a recommendation letter for another coaching position. I always ask him why and it just seems to me that he is just never content with what he has. One year, he was coming off a championship season and sent out a bunch of resumes for other coaching positions the following off-season. He has literally coached at so many different places that I wonder how he knows what hat to wear when he leaves the house. I'm a firm believer that at some point in your career you just have to say, this is where I am going to be. Commit to a program and do everything in your power to build it and make it into something special.

We live in such a society where instant gratification is so prominent that it makes you wonder if anyone ever works for a long-term goal anymore. Every year you see some big-time college coach leave for a fatter paycheck and you just wonder how you can blame a kid for leaving school early to cash in when he sees the adults around him doing the very same thing every day.

My brother always jokes with me when we get together for a family function, lunch, dinner, or something, by saying to me that he and his wife were asking each other which Berkshire Baseball shirt they thought that I may be wearing that day. He does it to make fun of me, the truth is that I take it as the biggest compliment that he could ever give me. It shows my loyalty and commitment to this organization. Kind of like Tommy Lasorda was to the Dodgers.

Sometimes I sit and think about the sacrifices that I have made over the years to continue to run a nonprofit amateur baseball organization, and I ask myself if it was worth it. For over twenty years, I've not been able to attend a family picnic on Memorial Day, July Fourth, or Labor Day because I've either been out of town at a baseball tournament or running a baseball tournament. My wife gets on me sometimes because I spend Father's Day and my birthday at the ballpark. We got married in January for two reasons, the first is that it was also the same date that we started dating, and the second was so that our anniversary wouldn't be in the middle of the baseball season. Had we not started dating in January, we probably never would have started dating in the first place, because starting a relationship during the baseball season would have been a disaster. Kind of similar to the theory in the movie *Fever Pitch*. I lured my wife into my life during the off-season so that once baseball season rolled around, she had already fallen madly in love with me and had to take the good with the bad.

I literally left a six-figure sales career in order to allow time to run a nonprofit organization, taking a pay cut of over $75,000 a year. Kind of makes me laugh when I hear people make a comment such as, "He does this for the money." I've spent more money out of my own pocket than anyone would to keep the organization afloat and at the end of the day, when someone asks me if it was worth it, without hesitation, the answer is "Yes!"

Now don't get me wrong, I am a human being and there are days when I can get frustrated and ask myself why I do what I do for so little in return, but the fact is that if I had the chance to do anything differently over the past twenty-one years, I wouldn't. This is truly a labor of love for me; I can't think of anything else that I would rather be doing than teaching kids about life through the game of baseball. If I touched the life of one player over all of these years, it would have all been worth it.

I used to have a picture taped on the wall of one of our 18-U team concession stands, a team photo with all the players' individual photos below it. On the very bottom of the pictures, I wrote, "This is why." It was kind of my own self-motivation for when I asked myself why I did what I did. I would usually get to the field on a tournament weekend between 5:00 and 6:00 a.m., get the field lined and ready to go and then head into the concession stand to start coffee and get things in order for whichever parents were working the first shift of the day. I'd look at that photo with that phrase written underneath it, and no matter what may have happened so far that morning, I stayed focused and reminded myself why I was there.

That's the thing with commitment; you can't make a commitment without making a sacrifice. You can't make a commitment without being loyal and you certainly can't make a commitment without being content. If you're always out there looking for the next best opportunity to come along, you'll never be able to commit to anything. You have to love what you do and love who you do it for or you will not be committed.

I once heard someone say that love is not a feeling; it's an act of your will. Commitment is the same way; it is a conscious decision and a conscious effort to sacrifice for the greater good.

I often think about how commitment and loyalty play such a large part in marriage as well. You have to be committed to each other in order for it to work. You have to take the good with the bad and still be willing to keep working. You can't approach your marriage as so many people approach their career and looking for the next best thing to come along. That contributes to our high divorce rates in this country. It goes back to our desire for instant gratification, lack of commitment, lack of loyalty, and not knowing how to be content. Again, at some point, you just have to make a decision that this is the person you're going to spend the rest of your life with, and then do whatever it takes to make that happen. I know that my wife could have certainly done better than having me for a husband, but for whatever reason, she is happy and content with me. If she was always out there looking for something better, she would have found it quite quickly, but she chose to stick with me and that's commitment. There is always going to be something better if you look hard enough, but at some point, you just have to make a conscious decision that you're going to play with the hand that you were dealt and make the best of it.

I know when I was in the building materials industry and we'd be looking to hire new employees, we would actually tell people that we were not interested in people who were looking for a new job, we were interested in people who were looking for a career. Plain and simple, the difference is commitment.

Every once in a while, I'll have someone tell me that they are very impressed with my Berkshire Baseball career coaching record and that I am the all-time wins leader in the history of the organization. When I was inducted into the Berkshire Baseball Hall of Fame in 2010, that same fact was mentioned during my induction ceremony. When I took the stage, I was quick to point out that I am not only the all-time wins leader for coaches in our organization's history, but also the all-time losses leader by losing over three hundred more games than the coach who is number two in the loss column. The over seven hundred wins come with almost five hundred losses to date. If I had to venture to guess, I would say that I was much more involved in the almost five hundred losses than I was in the over seven hundred wins. For most of the wins, I guess I was smart enough to stay out of the way of my players and let them play the game, for many of the losses, I'm going to guess that I probably got in the way and attempted to micromanage something during the course of the game and ended up screwing something up. However, the one thing that I am very proud of regarding my current 776-546-24 career coaching record with Berkshire Baseball is that it represents my commitment and loyalty to this organization. I've won and lost more games than any other coach in the organization simply because I have coached in more games than any other coach in the organization. It certainly is not because I'm the best coach in the organization. But again, for me what it symbolizes certainly makes me proud. I believe it speaks volumes about my character as an individual in that I have made a commitment to Berkshire Baseball for the long haul. I have had opportunities to go elsewhere to coach on occasion, but for the long-term outlook, I have made a commitment to stay here.

CHAPTER 7

Making Adjustments

When I was in sales, I would attend a ton of sales seminars. Every single one that I went to would tell me that they knew the secret to successful selling. So many of these seminars would give you an outline on how to be a successful salesman. They would all tell you that their way was the right way, the only way in some respects, that you could be successful in the sales industry. Many of them would give you a cookie-cutter approach, telling you that the same methods work for every customer that you will ever deal with. I always found that amazing and ridiculous at the same time; that they really believed that their way was one correct way to do something and that everyone else had it wrong. I prefer to go with the method that to be successful, whether it's in sales, baseball, or life, you have to know how to make adjustments. I never walked away from a sales seminar with the belief that I had just learned the secret to being successful. I was more of a believer in the theory that when I went to a sales seminar that I was searching for one or two things that I could use in my career. I wasn't looking for the gospel; I was looking for pieces to the puzzle. If I left a seminar with a few good ideas that I could use in my personal or professional life, I considered it time well spent.

I always went into a sales seminar with an open mind. I honestly never felt that I would go into a sales seminar and leave with all of the answers and all of the correct methods to sell and deal with customers. My philosophy was to go in and take what I could from everything that I had heard, and then use what I could for my customers and mold it into my own. I tell people when I speak publicly the same thing— that I am not going to give them all of the answers. Mainly, because I don't have all of the answers, nor will I ever have all of the answers. My goal when I speak to a group is that I can give everyone in the room one thing that they can remember and use in their lives. That one thing will be different for just about everyone in the room, but if they get just one thing from me, then I would consider my time with them as successful.

I coach with the same philosophy. The players who take more than just one thing—well, they end up being very special to a coach.

That's pretty much how I have approached my professional life and pretty much how I have approached my coaching career since I started. As a coach, you have to be a dime store psychologist. The method that you use to coach one team one year, may not work for another team the following year. I mean, of course your basic principles are not going to change, but each player, each team is going to have a different makeup. Your toughest job as a coach, as a supervisor, as a salesman, is figuring out what makes your "players" tick. How do you get through to them?

Some players you have to stroke and coddle a little bit more than others. Some players will respond to getting in their face every once in a while. You need to figure out what works for which kids and be able to know how to make the adjustment from one to another.

I remember hearing Pete Rose in an interview one time when asked what made him such a good hitter. He said it was all about knowing how to make adjustments. Whether hitting, pitching, or coaching, you have to be able to make an adjustment. Again, the basic principles and mechanics are always going to be the same but you need to know how to make that adjustment when you need to.

Hitters can't approach an at-bat against Josh Beckett in the same manner that they approach an at-bat against Tim Wakefield. By the same token, a coach can't use the same tones and mannerisms with a player like Kevin Youkilis and a player like J.D. Drew. It just doesn't work.

Yet every day, I see coaches get caught up in this cookie-cutter approach. They think that every hitter has to have a small stride, a long stride, no stride. Whatever their theory, they think that it is the only theory and they end up alienating their players and losing them.

If you watch the highlights on the *MLB Network* or *Baseball Tonight* on *ESPN* any given evening, you're going to see twenty-five different swings from twenty-five different Major League hitters. They all don't do it the same at the big league level, so why do so many youth coaches think that there is only one way to hit a baseball. Now again, the basic mechanics *are* the same. If you compare a bunch of big league hitters in still photographs at the point of contact, there really isn't much difference. How they get there is very different. That's what some coaches lose sight of. They have a hard time explaining to a young player that how they get to the point of contact isn't quite as important as making sure that they are correct at the point of contact. In their translation, they usually end up reserving to the fact that everything should be the same for every hitter. Again, they ultimately create some type of disconnect with the kid.

So many coaches lose sight of the fact that their players are truly human beings, they have feelings, opinions, and questions regardless of how old they are. Most importantly, they are all unique. Each one of them has his one little hot button and your biggest task is going to be to figure out what makes each of them tick. Coaching, like business and life, is all about relationships. How you relate to your players will determine how successful you will be as a coach.

I always tell my players that if something I tell them during a talk about hitting, fielding, base running, or anything doesn't make sense to them they need to ask me to explain it. You as coach need to be able to prove to players why you're telling them to do something a certain way. Make them feel comfortable in being able to ask you why. If you can't explain to a player why they should be doing something that you're telling them to do, then you shouldn't be telling them to do it that way in the first place. You have to be able to validate your theories.

Whenever I'm teaching at a camp or clinic, I always encourage the players to ask questions. I tell them that if something doesn't make sense to them that they need to ask me or any of our other instructors questions as to why we are telling them what we're telling them. I then go on to tell them to always ask questions if something doesn't make sense to them. Make sure that they are respectful when asking the question, but also make sure they understand why their coach or instructor is telling them to do this. I've seen many coaches actually get upset when a player asks the question, why? Me on the other hand, I encourage it. I want them to ask me questions because I realize that after twenty-plus years of coaching and teaching the game of baseball that I will sometimes assume that my students or players know something and I kind of skip over it. If you're a coach or teacher who doesn't encourage those you're leading to ask questions, to me that means that either you really do not understand why you're telling them to it that way or you're just trying to bluff your way through it. Either scenario is not good. If you can't explain to them why you're telling them to do something in a certain way, then you shouldn't be telling them to do it that way.

Why so many coaches feel that they can use a cookie-cutter method in teaching the game of baseball is really difficult for me to understand. There are no two people in the world that are the same, so why you would think that every player that you coach will respond to the same type of tactics seems odd to me. Again, the basic principles are going to be the same, but the approach is going to be a little different.

For the past several years, I've coached college-age players for about seventy-plus games over the summer. Then, immediately following the completion of that season, my 16-U team will start their fall season. I immediately have to make an adjustment as to how I approach those two different age groups. Everything has to be adjusted from the language that I use to communicate with them, to the general responsibility that I give them, to how we run the bases. They all require some tweaking. The principles, the fundamentals, the final goal will all remain the same; however, the path that we take to get there is going to be different. It can sometimes be a tiny adjustment, sometimes a big adjustment; nonetheless, an adjustment. You have to be able to make adjustments if you really want to be successful in this game. You have to know when to make the adjustments and you have to know when to keep your hands off as well; one is just as important as the other.

CHAPTER 8

Learning From Failure

*B*aseball is a game of failure. That again is one of the pure and natural beauties of the game itself. I said before, you can fail 70 percent of the time at the highest level of the game and you'll be enshrined with a bronze plaque of your face in Cooperstown. Just think about that. Think of any other profession in the world where you can screw up 70 percent of the time and still be considered the best at what you do. Other than a meteorologist, I honestly can't think of one. I often tell my players to really think about that. How eager would we be to hop on an airplane if we knew that an air traffic controller was going to get it right 30 percent of the time? I'm not a huge fan of flying to begin with and if I knew that there was 70 percent chance that I'd be flying into another airplane at thirty thousand feet, I can't say that I would have a real warm and fuzzy feeling about that. Baseball is such a wonderful game that it can allow you to fail and teach you valuable lessons from that failure. Most importantly, how to get back on your feet again, learn from that failure, and do something to correct it next time.

Life itself is full of failures. We all make mistakes, some more than others. People who are successful have all failed at some point in their lives. What makes them successful, what separates them from the average person is that they learn from their mistakes. They figure it out. They don't make the same mistake twice. As I said, the most successful people in the world failed. Some failed more than others, but they never let that failure knock them down. They knew how to take a punch. Life is going to throw all kinds crap at you on a daily basis, you need to deal with it and keep working toward your goals. The biggest thing that helps those in the world who are successful is that they are not afraid to fail. They are willing to take a chance, stick their necks out for something that they believe. They really are not afraid to fail because they realize that in the grand scheme of things, failure is oftentimes just another step on the ladder to success.

If you're afraid to fail, then you're approaching life in a very timid manner. If you're not willing to take a chance you'll never succeed. You can't go about your life always looking in the rearview mirror. You have to charge ahead and deal with the issues as they come. When you make a mistake, learn from it, and use it to help make you achieve your goal.

One of the toughest things to do in youth baseball today is getting kids to understand how to deal with failure. Some kids get so uptight when they fail that they end up compounding the problem by carrying that failure over into their next at-bat or out into the field on defense. Sometimes a player will confuse the concept of dealing with failure as actually accepting failure. Nothing could be further from the truth. You never want to accept failure, not on the baseball field or in life, but you do want to use it to your advantage, learn from it, and become stronger because of it. You can't let failing consume you. You have to deal with it and move on.

I had a player just a few years ago who was a perfectionist in every aspect of the word. He was a smart kid, a straight A student; he was almost perfect in everything else that he did, but on the baseball field he was not perfect. He was very talented, but certainly not perfect, as no one is. He had such a difficult time dealing with his failures on the baseball field that it was often actually painful to watch. There were actually so many times during this sixteen-year-old's season with me that I would have to pull him out of a game or pull him aside after a game and just try to calm him down. I tried being compassionate, I tried being the tough guy, I literally pulled out all of the stops on occasion and many times thought that I would never get through to him.

It was extremely frustrating for me as a coach because this kid had some real talent, but he would kill himself by beating himself up over a bad at-bat or not doing well. If his first at-bat of the game was not a quality at-bat in his mind, there was a good chance that he was done for the day. I would see him come up with a runner on third base with less than two outs and he would hit a deep fly ball or a ground ball to the right side to score the runner and he would come into the dugout like a madman who was fit to be tied, shouting that he sucked. I'd pull him to the side and say, "Hey, Mark, you just drove in a run. That's a good thing." This was an incredibly frustrating situation to deal with from a coaching standpoint. There were times when I just wanted to throw my hands up and say forget it, but I kept plugging away, I kept riding him, I kept telling him that he had to deal with his failures and channel that intensity and passion into positive energy, not negative energy. I wasn't about to give up on him, no matter how much he frustrated me at times. I always tell players, when I stop riding you, when I stop pushing you, that's when you need to worry, because it's only then when I have given up on you.

Even as our season ended, I wasn't completely convinced that I ever got through to him. However, as I've said over and over throughout this book, sometimes you have to wait for a little bit after you plant those seeds to actually see them harvested.

It wasn't until after he completed his 18-U season with our organization that I realized that he figured it out. I got the chance to see the fruits of my labor, I certainly wasn't the only one who helped Mark along the way, but I think that I had a little something to do with it. Our organization awards $2,000 in scholarships every year and as part of the scholarship application process, we ask each applicant to submit an essay with the scholarship application. The essay is to explain what impact participating in baseball or softball has had on applicants' lives and how they may be able to use those lessons in the future.

The essay that Mark Minisce submitted with his 2009 scholarship application was titled *"Baseball: The Art of Failure."* I feel compelled to share it with you here.

BASEBALL: THE ART OF FAILURE

Baseball has not only had a major impact on my life, but it has also prepared me for the future in ways that I could never have imagined. It has taught me skills that I could never learn anywhere else; not in the classroom, not in the community, and definitely not on my own. What I thought entered into my life as a sport, now has turned out to be my personal teacher. Baseball has taught me to do and be a lot of things; it has taught me sportsmanship, teamwork, and perhaps the most important of all, it has taught me how to accept failure.

One important lesson that baseball has taught me is to know my role and what part I am going to play in different situations. Sure this can be the same for everything I do, but in some cases there are not enough leaders and too many followers, and vice versa. Something that was very hard for me grasp even a year ago was how my role may change in different environments. Knowing your role and what you may be asked to accomplish at different times is all part of the team aspect of baseball. A goal can be defined as the result or achievement to which effort is directed. I believe that baseball helps kids learn how to be a part of a team, how to depend on others, and most important of all turn the result of the effort into achievement. What I find fascinating is this same principle that we all think is applying to baseball, applies to so much more than just that, whether it be in the classroom, on the field, or in the professional world, this idea of teamwork is everywhere.

Giving me exposure to different types of people, baseball has allowed me to bond with people having a common interest. Have you ever been near a dugout and wondered: What does all that mumble jumble that they're saying in there mean, and why don't I know what they're talking about? Something special happens when you see the same guys so often; you begin to form a type of bond with one another, known as camaraderie. Having the opportunity to play with a select few for years and years on end I was able to become really close to some of my teammates. This chance has allowed me, and the other select few to be able to allow our circle of comrades, if you will, to grow to eventually engulf most of the team. Growing this close to some has let me know that it is possible to meet new people, become friendly with them, and eventually almost always be supportive of them, when initially we only had one thing in common: interest in baseball.

Perhaps the most important "lessons" baseball has taught me is how to fail. Tougher than any professor I will ever have, harder than any boss I will ever work for, baseball, an unexpected mentor, taught me something that I would have never learned on my own. After about thirteen years, five of which I was playing about ten months per year, I am finally grasping the fact that I will not only fail at times, but on average about eight out of ten. I think this lesson was so hard for me to accept because I was not used to failing much of anything in my life up to this point. The fact that "straight A students" never experience failure completely had to be thrown out. Failing so much, I began to become exhausted with being frustrated and began feeling more optimistic and relaxed in pressure situations, and eventually began to succeed.

Has baseball made an impact on my life? Absolutely. By showing me how to be part of a team and getting to know people will definitely help in an environment where communication skills are crucial. Figuring out my role and how I can contribute for the good of a group will also help me in just about any group or class situation. Being part of many successful baseball teams has been an experience I will never forget, and I am thankful for the opportunities I had to be a part of them. Most important of all, the skills learned concerning failure and how to cope with disappointment will help me recover from major or minor setbacks that will occur in future college settings and the professional world.

~Mark Minisce

Berkshire Baseball
2009 Scholarship Recipient

Once again, I realized that if you're looking for instant gratification, then coaching certainly is not the line of work that you should get into. You need to understand that this is a labor of love and that you won't always see the fruits of your labor immediately. There were so many times during the two seasons that I coached Mark that I really felt as though I was completely wasting my time. Many times, I would say to myself, "This kid hates me and simply does not get it."

Again, patience always has to be the virtue. Over a year after the last game that I coached Mark Minisce in, I realized that he had listened to some of the things that I had told him after all. That was extremely rewarding.

CHAPTER 9

Playing The Game The Right Way

Playing the game the right way—what exactly does that mean? You hear it all the time, at every level of baseball, but does anyone really know what it means?

Well, I do have a few theories of my own that I'll share with you. Most of all, this entire book emphasizes various components of playing the game the right way.

In a nutshell, it means hustling all of the time, being focused, committed and dedicated and treating your teammates, opponents, officials and the game itself with respect.

Now, let's break each of those components down even further. Hustling all of the time; there is nothing that impresses a coach more than seeing a kid hustle. This is something that I can relate to quite a bit. As I said previously, I was an average baseball player at best when I played. Every time that I got onto the field, I hustled—period. The sole reason for me getting onto the field in the first place was because I hustled. I sprinted on and off the field. I loved to practice. When we'd practice, I would hustle all the time. I'd dive for balls in practice, I'd get dirty at practice and I'd work up a good sweat at practice. Nothing in the world can make up for hustle. Baseball's all-time leader in hits, Pete Rose, was nicknamed Charlie Hustle. If you asked most of the guys who played with or against Rose in his career they would tell you that he was never the most talented guy on the field, but what he lacked in talent, he made up for in guts, grit. and hustle. He played hard all the time, whether it was the first game of the season or the seventh game of the World Series, he went all out.

In a game of failure, hustling is the one thing in baseball that you can actually do right 100 percent of the time. You can't get a base hit every time you come to the plate, you can't field every ball hit to you, but you can hustle 100 percent of the time. It kind of makes you wonder why in a game that is so entrenched in failure would you not want to do the one thing that you can do correctly all the time?

As a coach, those are the guys you love. I like to call them "dirtbags" or "dirt balls." Those are the guys who are pissed at themselves at the end of the game if their uniform is still clean. In their minds, they think that they didn't contribute if they are not covered in dirt at the end of the day. Our organization gives out an award every year called the Sportsmanship/Hustle Award. Give me nine guys that win that award every year and I'll bring home a lot of wins.

Since I've been coaching, I've instituted a rule for my players to sprint on and off the field every inning of every game. No exceptions. I simply tell them that they can give me fourteen sprints during the game or fourteen sprints after the game; the choice is theirs. We've instituted that rule as a must throughout our organization; however, we need to do a better job of getting every single coach to enforce it better. We still have some coaches who will let a kid slide if he loafs every once in a while. That needs to change. We're still working on that.

A few years ago, we were at a tournament in Myrtle Beach, South Carolina, with our 16-U team. We had a group that was very talented, but quite frankly underachieved as a group. In fact, it's the same group of kids that I alluded to earlier in the book who won their only tournament the same week that I had lost my job. This was our final weekend of the season and we once again were underachieving. We were sitting at 0-3 on the weekend and were waiting to play our final game of the season, a consolation game. We had already guaranteed ourselves our first losing season in quite some time and now this last game would only determine whether we would finish the year one game or two games below the .500 mark. I sat there on the ball bucket watching the two teams play in the game before us lamenting the fact that we under-achieved and venting to my assistant coach as to what we as a coaching staff could have done differently to better prepare the team to play.

All of the sudden the tournament director came up to us and com-plimented us on how nice a team we had. At first, I wanted to smack him because I certainly felt that we had a nice team, but I also felt for sure that at 0-3 and waiting for the consolation game to start, we had not shown our true colors this weekend.

As the director continued to talk to us, he commented on the fact that he was very impressed with how our team hustled. He said, "Even at 0-3, your kids never stopped sprinting on and off the baseball field, that's really nice to see at this level."

My demeanor immediately changed, about the weekend and the season. I realized that even though we came up much shorter than our expectations for the season, the kids bought into hustling on every play and that made me proud. Wins and losses aside, they were playing the game the right way and that was truly the biggest request that we had made of them at the beginning the season. We always tell them, learn how to play the game the right way and the wins and losses will be taken care of on their own.

Sometimes coaching is like farming; you plant the seed and hope that you can harvest a good crop. Sometimes though, the crop takes longer to blossom than what you might think and you personally may not get to reap the harvest. The main thing to remember though is that as long as someone gets to reap the harvest, then you did your job as a coach. With that team in particular we didn't get to reap the harvest, but it certainly ended up being a very good crop.

Earlier in the book, I mentioned them. The following year, when that same core group of kids moved up to play on our 18-U team, they were the team that had finally came into their own. They went on a tear into the final two weeks of their 18-U season and won their final two tournaments of the year, including the prestigious LVBA Desert Fall Classic, the national caliber tournament in Las Vegas, Nevada, in their season finale. I was very proud of them as I watched them celebrate from the stands that night, hoping that they had learned something from us as a coaching staff in the previous two seasons that led to their success on this night.

I had touched on being focused all the time earlier as well. But again, just like working on the fundamentals, I like to drive my point home sometimes.

The crop of kids that had underachieved as fifteen- and sixteen-year-olds blossomed in that final year. This was a group of kids that when we would travel, you could bet your bottom dollar, one of them would do something to get them to run sprints. Miss curfew, sneak into another buddy's room after bed check to play poker, you name it they probably tried it. But when they got to be seniors during their 18-U season, it was like they finally "got it." They were focused, a group that traditionally played poorly on road trips because they were more concerned about picking up chicks and being the top goofball of the weekend, finally realized that when they traveled, they were there to play baseball and to represent the Berkshire Baseball and Softball Club. Once they finally realized that, they did some special things as a team. They won their final eleven games and two tournaments, all while on road trips in Rehoboth Beach and Las Vegas. Although I wasn't on the field with them for that final season, I was proud to have been able to influence them the previous two years.

Being focused just simply means to concentrate on the task at hand 100 percent. No matter what else is going on in your life, you need to stay focused. You need to zone everything else out while you are between the lines in a game or at practice. Again, I don't care whether it is baseball or your career, you have to know when and how to "check your problems at the door." That is so important, yet extremely difficult as well. To tell a kid who just left a house where his mom and dad were fighting and are on the brink of a divorce to forget about that for two to three hours can be a daunting task, but those who can do that are the ones who rise above it and come to the top.

As a coach, you have to make your players buy into the theory of making baseball their own personal sanctuary. You have to relay to them that baseball can be an escape and a place where everything can be perfect if they allow it to. Frankly, some players will just never get it. They're involved for all of the wrong reasons. Whether they're just there because Mom and Dad want them there or to kill time, who knows, but they will eventually weed themselves out and as a coach you still need to try to reach them regardless of how frustrating that may be at times. You can't write them off until they write themselves off. The thing you have to realize as a coach when you come across those players that are just going through the motions is that you can still teach them some valuable life lessons while they are under your tutelage. Those are the players who ten, fifteen, twenty years down the road, will finally get it. You may never know it, but they will. That is the one thing about coaching that some people can't grasp. If you are doing it for some sort of quick self-gratification, you're going to come up empty. That's the point that many coaches don't get, they think that at the end of the day, people are going to remember their record, the number of wins and the number of losses, but truthfully they're not. The players will remember you as a coach for who you are, not for how many games you won or lost. When a coach goes out there with a win-at-all-cost attitude; the coach has missed the point. To have a pitcher throw a ridiculous number of pitches so that you can win a championship is both selfish and shortsighted. To win a game or a championship at the expense of a kid's health is ludicrous, yet it happens every day in youth baseball across America.

My younger cousin, Scott Kramer, who was drafted by the Cleveland Indians in the thirteenth round of the Major League Baseball draft in 1994, once had a coach of his send him out to throw 194 pitches in an American Legion play-off game. The next day, our local newspaper glorified the incident, by stating that Scott's "gutsy 194 pitch performance" helped lead his team into the county championship game. I was at the game and watched in disbelief as the coach continued to send this seventeen-year-old kid to the mound inning after inning and then was completely baffled the next day when our local newspaper didn't seem to think that there was anything wrong with what happened the night before. I've often asked myself, was winning that game so important that an adult would completely risk the welfare of a child's arm to make it to the championship game? I honestly don't get it. Is that why we coach?

Was that really in the best interest of the kid? What life lessons were taught on that night? That winning a summer baseball game was worth risking a kid's arm? Again, I'm sorry if I'm beating a dead horse here, but even now almost twenty years later, it just doesn't make sense to me.

That's not teaching kids to play the game the right way, that's simply teaching them that winning is the most important thing and nothing else matters.

Being dedicated and committed is another fine line that we have to teach as coaches without going overboard. You need to stress to your players that they have to be dedicated, but you need to be realistic as well, making sure that they prioritize correctly. Being completely dedicated to baseball but never going to class certainly isn't a very balanced approach.

You need to explain to your players that if they're going to succeed not only on the baseball diamond, but also in life, that they will need to be dedicated to their craft and work hard. They also need to understand that if they have a choice between taking ten rounds of batting practice and completing their ten-page term paper that is due tomorrow, that they need to choose the latter or they probably need to reevaluate their priorities. Your entire life is about choices. Every day we make hundreds of choices, some have a much larger effect on us then others; nonetheless, we are always making choices. We're not always going to make the correct choices. How we react to the wrong choices that we make oftentimes defines who we are as human beings.

Being dedicated means loving to be there. If you are dedicated, then getting up early to go to practice is not a chore. You want to be there. You want to work hard and you want to get better. I like to compare it to a labor of love. It's hard work, but you never get tired of it because you love the game. That is truly what dedication and commitment are all about.

As I had said earlier, I always like to refer to the chicken and the pig when I tell players about commitment. If they look at baseball as a bacon-and-egg breakfast platter, both a chicken and a pig took part in making that breakfast what it is. The chicken is involved with the breakfast, but the pig is committed. Again, I am looking for a bunch of pigs when I am recruiting players. I want guys who are dedicated and committed and love to be at the ballpark.

Billy Ripken had mentioned something to me when he spoke at our organization's annual banquet back in January of 2008 that really hit home for me. He told me that when he was growing up, his father, Cal Ripken Sr., would only take him and his brother, Cal Jr., to the ballpark if they asked to go. Here was a man who had spent his entire life involved in the game of baseball who I am sure, like any other dad, wanted his kids to take up the American pastime. Yet he was level-headed enough to make sure that it was something that his kids wanted to do, not something that he was forcing his kids to do. What a great lesson that is for every parent, support your children in every way that you can, but ultimately let them decide what they want to do.

I've mentioned several times earlier a saying my mom shared with me as I became a parent and I think of it all of the time. She once told me, "God only requires me to do two things as a parent, teach my children how to walk and teach my children how to walk away. The second one is much harder than the first."

Truer words have never been spoken. Sometimes we just need to be smart enough to allow our kids to make a few mistakes and see what they learn from those mistakes.

The final component of playing the game the right way is treating your teammates, opponents, and officials with respect. I touched on this earlier as well. Respect is something that is earned. If you are a good teammate and treat your coaches, teammates, and the officials with respect, you in turn will earn their respect. You can be competitive and be a good sport as well. Some people don't think that players who conduct themselves with dignity and class are competitive. I find that very disturbing. You can play the game hard and put everything you have into striving to be the best person on the field and still be a good and respectful teammate.

The best players lead by example. They play hard every inning and they pick their teammates up when they make a mistake—not by belittling them, but by taking them under their wing and leading the way.

Those players that rise above the rest can beat opponents without embarrassing them or talking trash. The players who learn how to play the game the right way can earn an opponent's respect by simply hustling and playing the game in a businesslike manner. Let your play do the talking and keep your mouth shut. If you hit a home run, act like you've done it before, get around the bases and back into the dugout. Don't show up the pitcher. If you make a big play in the field, just get ready for the next play. The game is relatively simple: hit, run, and throw. Celebrate after the game, not after every good play. You are supposed to make the plays during the game; that's your job. There is no reason to celebrate during the game. Sure, the game is driven by emotions and when there is a game-shifting event, guys are going to get excited about it. Just make sure that you keep it in perspective. Too much celebrating during the course of the game can be considered as disrespectful to your opponents. The term "let sleeping dogs lie" can be very useful in the game of baseball. You never want to do something so disrespectful to your opponents that it gives them a reason to come back.

Treating officials with respect goes hand in hand with treating your teammates, coaches, and opponents with respect as well. You should always refer to the umpire as "sir" or "Mr. Umpire." Realize that they really do not have a vested interest in the outcome of the game and that they too are human beings. They will make mistakes. Treat them respectfully and they will treat you the same way. If you stand out in the field or sit in the dugout yelling and screaming about every call, I can pretty much guarantee you that the first close questionable call is not going to go your way. In fact, as a player, there really is never any reason to argue with an umpire about anything—period. If your coach truly believes that an injustice was done by the umpire, he is the one—and the only one—who should address the umpire. Believe me there are ways as a coach when you can respectfully question an umpire's call without making him feel that you are trying to intimidate him or show him up. Again, common sense is the main factor here though. Think about how you would wish to be questioned if you may made a mistake and use that same approach with the umpire. More than likely, the call isn't going to change anyway, but if you speak in a respectful manner, that will go a long way in the game of respect that you have just earned from that umpire.

The theory of trying to intimidate an umpire into making calls for you is idiotic, to be quite frank about it. Believe it or not though, coaches have told me that if they ride the umpire from the very first pitch that he'll start calling the game their way. Again, this theory is bizarre to me. For people to actually think that they could publicly embarrass another person enough to make him call the game their way is just a bit off kilter in my eyes. Personally, I have always found the exact opposite to be true. Intimidating or bullying an umpire is usually a surefire way to get you sent to the showers rather quickly.

Again, I fully realize that we're all human and sometimes even the best, most respectful, individual may lose his composure. The key, however, is to make those times the exception, not the norm. I've questioned umpires in a respectful manner and on occasion I have lost my cool a bit. The times when I have lost my cool, I truly felt like a jackass afterward. Whether I was right or wrong I lost my composure and that was unacceptable. The main problem is that some coaches take pride in that type of behavior and at the end of the day when the heat of competition is over, they still do not feel as though they acted inappropriately. It certainly is not the way to set an example for a young man when you are trying to be a role model.

Twice in my twenty-plus years of coaching baseball, I have been ejected from a game, I am not proud of that statistic. Both times, I will tell you that I still believe I was right in my argument with the umpire. Both times, I deserved to be ejected. Both times, I am sure that I looked like a complete jackass to the fans and players who saw the outbursts. What I guess I am proud of is the fact that I am man enough to admit that my actions were wrong and the result of my actions was deserved. To hear coaches talk about and truly boast about times that they were tossed with no type of remorse whatsoever disturbs me. If you are going to be an example and a role model to kids, then you need to be man enough to admit when you are wrong.

You'll hear many people say "respect the game," and what exactly does that mean? Baseball is one sport that has a very long lineage of tradition and structure. When you get right down to it, the game itself has not changed very much since the 1800s. Treat the game with respect, almost as if you need to really understand the history of the game of baseball. Respect those who have gone on before you and played.

Looking good when you step onto the field, looking good when you get to the field, making sure that your shirt is tucked in, your hat is on straight, all that sort of stuff goes hand in hand with treating the game with respect. I have a very old-school approach when it comes to the game of baseball. I heard Larry Bowa comment on being considered old school once, and he said there is no old school, there is no new school; the game is baseball and it should be played the correct way.

When coaches can teach their players to go about their business on the baseball field in a professional manner and can get their players to buy in to hustling all of the time, being focused, committed and dedicated, and treating teammates, opponents, and officials with respect, then everybody that is involved in the game is much better off.

CHAPTER 10

Tough Love

One of the many things that my mother taught me during her short time here on earth was tough love. It's a concept that many people have a difficult time grasping nowadays. We have developed into a society where parents feel that the best way to love their children is to give them everything they want, let them do whatever they want, and never ever discipline them, for it may harm their precious little ego and self-confidence. That same attitude has started to roll over into sports as well. More and more dads are coaching their kids so that they can make sure that little Johnny is in the starting lineup every day and is batting third. Tough love is nonexistent because most coaches nowadays are there for one kid, their own, instead of the entire team. It's tough for them to establish any type of rules or disciplinary practices because they are there for all of the wrong reasons.

My mom had a tough life growing up. Her parents split up when she was very young and she actually ended up raising several of her siblings. As she grew up, things didn't get much easier. She was a tough woman who had no problem telling you when you did something wrong. She also cared in a very special way about those who were around her.

She decided to go back to college in her forties to earn a degree as a drug and alcohol counselor. This decision was based largely on the effect that my stepfather's alcoholism had on the demise of her second marriage as well as her own father's alcoholism.

As her new career started, her theory on tough love was brought to new levels. She ran a halfway house for women in recovery and it was her job to keep them sober and reintegrate them into society. She had to be tough enough to come down hard on them when they needed it, yet soft enough to reach out and give them a hug and cry with them when they needed it as well.

My mom had to teach me my own lesson in tough love when I was a teenager. I was fourteen years old at the time, my mom and dad had already divorced and I had been living in Palm Bay, Florida, with my mom for the previous four years. A couple of friends of mine and I thought that it would be a pretty neat idea to have a couple of beers and then go into a local convenience store where two of us distracted the clerk in the back of the store while the other one opened the cash register and took the money out. At the time it sounded like a flawless plan, unfortunately the fact that both the clerk and the owner of the convenience store knew all of us kind of threw a wrench into the scheme. I guess what we didn't think through was the clerk, not being born yesterday, wouldn't have a very tough time figuring out where the money went, considering the register had money in it prior to us stopping by and then had nothing in it but change when the first customer after us stopped in. I found out fast that beer, fourteen, and criminal activity were a recipe for disaster.

A few days later, I was leaving to go visit my dad in Pennsylvania for the summer. As I got on the plane to head north, I figured that I was scot-free. Shortly after I arrived in Pennsylvania, I received a phone call from my mother. The conversation started out well enough and then took a dramatic turn for the worse when she said, "By the way, I stopped down at the Minute Market today and saw Mike..."

My heart dropped into my stomach. I was completely speechless as she went on to tell me that he wasn't going to report the incident to the police as long as we all made restitution. This came as somewhat of a relief until she told me that what the other kids' parents did was up to them, but that she had already taken the full amount out of my personal savings account and paid it back. I thought, "What the hell, I only got a third of the money, why did I have to pay the whole thing back?" Unfortunately for me, there was no negotiating with her on this one. This little act of stupidity had just cost me three times what I got out of it. Then she dropped the bomb on me, and I will never forget what she said next. "Danny," she said, "you've gotten way too out of control for me anymore. You won't be coming back to live with me in Florida. You're going to be staying with your dad from now on."

I honestly thought that my world had ended. Nothing against my father, I loved him dearly, but seriously, my world had just been turned upside down. To leave all of your friends in the summer and then all of a sudden realize that you're not going back was quite a blow to a fourteen-year- old boy.

Obviously, this wasn't the first time that I had gotten into trouble. My mom truly did give me several chances, but she knew that I was flirting with disaster. I was in eighth grade and truly heading down a dark path. I was hanging out with the wrong set of friends and quite simply just being a punk. I truly believe today that had my mother not made that decision and exercised tough love on me, either I would be dead or in jail today, which is a fact.

At the time, I hated my mother for doing that to me. I made sure that I told everyone around me how cruel she was and how she didn't really love me. The truth was that she loved me so much that she knew what I needed most. That is truly the definition of tough love—to love someone so much, that you make a decision that is best for them, no matter how much it breaks your own heart.

I know now that is what I did to my mom that day. I broke her heart and she was strong enough to turn that into a good thing for me.

Even at the age of fourteen, I knew the truth, no matter what I had told other people. I got what I deserved—actually I got off better than what I should have. I knew that deep down inside.

Obviously, as I stated in my dedication at the beginning of this book, my relationship with my mother improved drastically as I grew older. I realized what she did and why. I realized that every decision she ever made in her life was always with someone else's best interest in mind.

Later in my life, I still remember a conversation that I had with her on the phone, amazingly enough, she had turned into my greatest confidant. At the time I was venting to her how I was having a tough time with my daughter, who was a teenager now and I just couldn't seem to relate to her at all. She told me that sometimes you have to be a good enough parent to let your kids make their own mistakes.

That was the first time that she had told me that God only required me to do two things as a parent, teach my children how to walk and teach them how to walk away. The first one is a whole lot easier than the second.

I still don't know if she came up with that one on her own or if she read it in a book or heard it from somewhere else, but I will never ever forget that. Both as a parent and as a coach, our talk on the phone that day did me a world of good. Boy do I ever miss those talks.

I know that I've used that phrase multiple times in this book, but if you're a parent and there is one thing that you should take away from this book, that is it. It goes back to the "spring training theory"; drive home the fundamentals until they just come naturally.

Every good coach has to be a disciplinarian as well. You have to establish early in the season that you are in charge. Players will test you from the start, regardless of what level you're coaching at, to see what they can get away with, that is simply human nature. When I talk about being a disciplinarian, I'm not necessarily talking about "ruling with an iron first." I simply mean establishing a chain of command and sticking to it.

Sometimes people think that when a coach is referred to as a "players' coach" that he allows his players to run rampant without any rules. There may be nothing further from the truth. A "players' coach" establishes the rules early and then sticks to them. His rules are the same for every player on the team, whether it's the top star on the team or the twenty-fifth guy. In fact, a players' coach oftentimes will hold his star players to a higher standard and expect them to lead by example. A players' coach is a coach who stands behind his players and supports them in every aspect of the game. He is the first guy off the bench to congratulate them on a nice play. He is the first guy off the bench to pick them up after they make a mistake, but he is also the first guy off the bench to tell them when they have screwed up. His discipline is handled on a man-to-man basis. He does not embarrass a player who has not already embarrassed himself. He understands the importance of explaining and communicating with his players the reason for his actions. Therefore, his players earn his respect, and understand up-front the consequences of their actions if they choose to not follow the letter of the law as the coach has established it.

You can never dismiss the fact that as a coach you are in that position to teach your players not only how to play the game on the field, but much more importantly, you are there to teach them how to conduct themselves off the field as well. Those coaches who put winning ahead of discipline by allowing their star players to get away with anything and everything and never holding them accountable for their actions are weak men and poor leaders.

A coach who does not discipline his players will quickly lose control of his team. As I said earlier, respect is earned; a coach without discipline will never earn the respect of his players.

Once you establish the rules, you have to enforce them. The first time a player breaks one of those rules, regardless of who he is, you have to act swiftly and enforce your law. If you do nothing after the first violation, you will lose all of your players' respect and slowly start to lose control of your team.

When players realize that you are serious about your rules of discipline, they will fall into line quickly. After the first incident where you bench a star player for tossing a helmet or not hustling, believe me, the rest of the team will quickly understand who the boss is. On the other hand, if you establish a set of double standards from the outset, you are quickly setting yourself up for a fall.

Make an example of one of your lower-echelon players and then do absolutely nothing when one of your top-tier players breaks the same rule—you've gained nothing and taught your team that if you throw hard or you are the best hitter on the team that you can do anything that you want. You've effectively established a double standard.

Sometimes when I talk about discipline, people think that you have to be a miserable human being to be a disciplinarian, which is hardly the case. As a coach, you are often the "second parent" to your players. You have to view them as your own children. To discipline your child does not mean that you do not love them. It is the same for your players. It's what I like to refer to as tough love. It's that type of love where you love others and care for them enough that you can tell them when they screw up. You can make them understand that there are consequences for every decision that they make in life. Sometimes those consequences are positive, sometimes they are negative. It's all part of the decision-making process in life. Every day people have to make thousands of decisions, and every decision that we make sets off a chain reaction of several other decisions. As human beings we're never going to make all of the correct decisions, no one is above that simple truth; however, it is how you react to the incorrect decisions that you make in your life that will define you as a human being.

Baseball is a game about failure. Fail 70 percent of the time and you're considered pretty damn good. What makes you successful as a baseball player is the exact same thing that will make you successful as a human being—how you react to those failures and what you learn from your mistakes.

As a player, if you break one of the coach's rules and get called out for it, you have to be man enough to sit back and look at the big picture; admit your mistake and accept the consequences. The one thing that I found out early in my life is that you can lie to a lot of people in the world, but you can never lie to that man in the mirror. You can certainly try to, but you will never succeed. You can try to tell your wife, your girlfriend, your teammates, and your parents that the coach was just picking on you or something to that effect, but late at night, before you go to bed, can you look yourself in the mirror and still tell that same lie? That is the moment of truth for every human being.

I learned a lot about the character of Jimmy Rollins of the Philadelphia Phillies during their 2008 season. There was a game on June 5, 2008, where he didn't hustle and his manager, Charlie Manuel, pulled him out of the game. After the game, Rollins was asked about the incident and Jimmy was man enough to make the following statement regarding what happened: "There is no explanation, I just didn't do it, and sometimes, the manager gets you. I know better. I'll just go out there and make sure I don't do it again. He's the manager, and that's what he's supposed to do. He has two rules: One, be on time. Two, Hustle. I broke one of them."

When asked if he was upset with Manuel's discipline, Rollins said he wasn't. "It's like breaking the law and getting mad when the police show up," he said. "He's been here four years, and we've probably talked about it twice. Three strikes and you're out, I guess. I'm not going to be a distraction. This is his team. I did what I did. When you do something, you get caught, and it is what it is. Problems only occur when they keep reoccurring."

Now that was the sign of a true man right there. Admitting that he made a mistake and simply accepting the consequences for it. Too often, we see on *Sports Center* and in the papers a professional player who gets benched and then calls out his coach or manager about the situation. Jimmy Rollins showed me personally that day his true character. We need more players in the professional ranks to step up and publically accept the consequences for their actions when they are disciplined. That goes back to that whole role model concept; the more guys in those positions who make the decision to be accountable for their actions, the more kids who will understand accountability as they grow up. Whether you're a professional athlete who was just benched by your coach or a fourteen-year-old kid who was just told by your mother that you're being sent to live somewhere else, you need to be able to reach deep down inside your heart of hearts and admit that you got what you deserved.

By the same token, whether you are a coach or a parent, you need to realize that your true task in life, on and off the baseball field, is to teach your children, whether a child by blood or through your team, how to function and make the correct decisions in their lives after we are gone.

Always remember, God requires us to do only two things as parents, teach your children how to walk and teach them how to walk away. The first one is going to be a whole lot easier than the second.

Charlie Manuel is considered a players' coach and he is, but he also knew that he needed to discipline his star player in order to keep the respect of the rest of his team, proving that he truly is a players' coach and a great leader.

CHAPTER 11

The Game Is Colorless

I have been fortunate enough to be raised by some very well-rooted individuals in both my mother and father. They taught me from a very young age that human beings should be judged by who they are, not by the color of their skin. Baseball, the game itself is completely colorblind. It will treat you the same whether you are white, black, American, Hispanic, Japanese—it doesn't matter. If you have talent, if you throw the baseball well, if you hit a baseball well, if you can field or if you can run, you can be successful in this game. On the other hand, if you do not have that talent, you will not be successful, regardless of the color of your skin.

Babe Ruth didn't hold the career home run record for five decades because he was white; he held it because he was the best at the time. When Hank Aaron broke that record, it was because he was now the best at that time, not because he was black. Barry Bonds broke Hank Aaron's record because he hit more home runs than Hank Aaron did, not because he was a black man. The game itself had no prejudice; it rewarded whoever the best *man* was at that time—period.

Granted, we as a society had a very hard time grasping that concept up until the great Jackie Robinson made his Major League debut on April 15, 1947. It took quite awhile for the concept to catch on, but once it did, again the game itself took over and held no prejudice whatsoever. If you were good, you were good, it didn't matter what color your skin was or where you were born.

That is another one of the great things about this game. It is pure. If you have what it takes to succeed on the field, you will, regardless of the color of your skin.

This is a great lesson that the game can teach us if we all just allow it to. During his Hall of Fame induction speech, Bruce Sutter said, "The game of baseball is perfect, but the people who play it are not." The game truly is perfect in every sense of the word. It is perfect in the fact that it is timeless, the field is perfectly square, and at the end of the game the scoreboard doesn't lie. It is perfect in the fact that if you work hard and stay focused you will be successful, regardless of the color of your skin.

I have personally always struggled with the entire concept of black versus white and prejudice as a whole; I honestly just don't get it.

My dad told me a story that when I was in preschool, one of my best friends was black. He told me that after a few weeks he had asked me if I was still playing with my friend Kevin, the black boy. Apparently, I gave him some sort of odd look when he asked me and he asked me again, "Kevin," He said, "Isn't that the name of your black friend in school?" He then said that my response stunned him, when I said, "My friend is Kevin, but I'm not sure if he is black, I will have to check tomorrow and let you know." Now I personally do not remember this story, but I am very proud of it. I guess you can chalk this up to "the wisdom of a child." Again, I am extremely thankful to both of my parents for teaching me from a very young age that the color of people's skin does not make them who they are. My parents worked and socialized with a complete melting pot of humanity and I can honestly say that I cannot ever remember my parents treating people differently because of the color of their skin. They taught me that people are people, plain and simple. We all have the same feelings and long to be accepted simply for who we are.

On the field, some of my best teammates and players had a darker skin tone than mine. I never thought of them differently and I never treated them differently. They were some of the best people that I have ever known in my life. I have always taken the approach that if you are a good person, with decent qualities, I am going to like you. I have met white people who are great individuals and I have met white people who are quite honestly lousy human beings. The same goes for black people, Hispanics, Asians, doesn't matter. The thing is, I have always made those determinations after speaking to the individuals and learning about them and their character. The color of their skin was never a determining factor.

I remember playing in a tournament in 1992 with our Berkshire Red Sox adult team, which was comprised of guys whose ages were anywhere from seventeen to thirty in Unionville, Pennsylvania, which was a small town just outside of State College, Pennsylvania. Players' ages ranged from a few kids who were still in high school to a guy whose professional career had just come to an end earlier that spring.

This was one of the few times that I had really seen prejudice firsthand. You have to understand, I went to a middle school in Melbourne, Florida, where 70 percent of the student population was black, and I had never experienced what I experienced on that baseball field that day. I'm not sure if I just had blinders on for so many years or what, but this was heartbreaking for me to witness.

We had two black players on our team that year, Erron Archie and Tony Hardy, two of the most naturally athletic and talented individuals that I had ever met. They were also two of the nicest kids that I had ever coached. Tony was only seventeen years old and Erron was nineteen. We were in a quarterfinal game in the single elimination tournament and we were playing the Howard Hawks, a team from the local league that was hosting the tournament and we were on their home field.

Erron was pitching and, frankly, he was unstoppable on this particular day. He threw in the upper 80s and had some very raw talent. I had always told him that he reminded me of Oil Can Boyd because he was a tall, skinny, lanky kid with long arms and legs. His philosophy was simply to throw the ball past you. Here is my fastball, try to hit it, was his theory.

Frustration was starting to get the best of the Howard team so they resorted to racial slurs. Somewhere in about the fifth inning or so, Erron came to the plate with a runner on second. Some of what we had actually thought at the time were fans of the Howard team were sitting in the bleachers behind home plate and started calling Erron the N-word and "boy" as he stepped up to the plate. Obviously, Erron was not impressed with the lack of class and hospitality that they were showing to him, so he stepped out of the batter's box for a few seconds and exchanged a few words with the fans. To my amazement, the umpire said nothing to the fans but ordered Erron to get into the batter's box. I was coaching first base at the time and before the Howard pitcher delivered the first pitch of the at-bat, I looked over into our dugout and noticed that every single member of our team was standing on the top step of our dugout in anticipation of what was about to happen. I then looked into the Howard dugout and noticed that their team was doing the same. Obviously, what happened next was no surprise to anyone there with the apparent exception of the umpiring crew.

As everyone had expected, the first pitch of the at-bat landed squarely in the middle of Erron's back. The benches cleared and we all were out there pushing and shoving for about fifteen minutes or so. Erron actually somehow ended up in the stands and to my amazement, not one player was ejected during the incident—not Erron, not the pitcher that threw at him, not me, no one. It was really quite astonishing. As we pleaded with the umpire that this was an obvious intentional drilling of our player and that the Howard pitcher should be ejected, he insisted that he had known the pitcher since he was a young boy and that he knew that he would never throw a pitch at a batter intentionally, even if he was black. That made me sick to my stomach in its own right. I just couldn't believe how a man of authority could simply ignore what had just happened. Once order was restored, I walked back to the first base coaching box with my arm around Erron on his way to first convincing him that no matter what, he could not retaliate once he got back onto the mound. He had to keep his cool and be the bigger man. Here I was telling Erron to be the bigger man and turn the other cheek, while at the same time I was thinking to myself, if I were on the mound the next inning, somebody would be wearing one.

As I walked with him, with my arm around him trying to calm him down, several thoughts were rushing through my head. My first thought, was again, amazement, that what had just happened didn't result in any player being ejected from the game and the umpire's obvious racism.

I also couldn't fathom that in the year 1992 in Central Pennsylvania, I had just witnessed racism in its truest form. On the other hand, I also felt very proud that the players on our squad were man enough to rise above racism and accept our teammates for who they were as human beings. For sixteen white guys to come to the defense of our black teammate was actually quite impressive in the midst of the ugliness that had raised its head that day.

As it turned out, Erron took the mound the next inning and, low and behold, our opponent's pitcher was leading off the inning. I was once again proud of the fact that this young nineteen-year-old kid rose above the prejudice that was surrounding him and threw the guy three straight fastballs on the outside corner of the plate that the batter weakly waved at before heading back to the dugout.

With everything that had happened up until that point, I don't think that any one of us would have blamed Erron if he had drilled that guy on the first pitch of the at-bat. However, Erron realized what was at stake. He knew what our pitching staff looked like for the remainder of the tournament and he knew that if we were going to win the title, we'd have to play three games that day. He knew we needed him to stay in the game and he realized that if he threw one pitch anywhere near one of their players that the racist umpire behind the plate was going to eject him without question. So at that moment in time, this young nineteen-year-old kid realized that the goals of the team were more important to him than his own personal feelings.

We went onto to win the game, and Erron pitched a complete game. We won our semifinal game and we then advanced to the championship game, where we lost to North Berwick 7-6 in what was our third game of the day. As we arrived at the next field for our semifinal game against the host, Unionville Cardinals, the tournament director came up to us in our van and apologized for what had happened over at the other field. He then informed us that it was actually three of his players, not fans from the Howard team, who were in the stands and started the whole incident by using the racial slurs toward Erron to begin with. Apparently, they were there to scout the game and they let their prejudice get the best of them. He also informed us that none of those players would be playing in the game against us or in the championship game if they happened to beat us in the semifinal. After everything that had happened so far that day, this was a breath of fresh air. This coach was man enough to discipline three of his players and prevent them from playing in a semifinal game. At that point, we truthfully had no idea that any of his players were even involved in the incident. Had their coach not mentioned anything to us, we would not have had any idea. This coach put teaching his players a very important life lesson ahead of winning, and I commend him for that even to this day.

I learned quite a few things that day about the makeup of our team, about the makeup of myself and about the makeup of two very fine young men named Erron Archie and Tony Hardy. I was proud to see the way our fledgling organization rallied around Erron, as an obvious injustice had been committed toward one of our teammates. I was proud of myself that I was still color-blind to a person's skin tone and that my parents had obviously succeeded in their attempt to teach me to judge a man by his character and not the color of his skin. Most of all, I was proud of Erron Archie and Tony Hardy who proved to me that at the tender ages of nineteen and seventeen, respectively, that they were able to rise above the obvious prejudice that had surrounded them that day and stay focused on the game. They both put their personal feelings aside, continued to focus on the game, and understood that the team goals were what they wanted to focus on, not their personal feelings.

I commend Major League Baseball for starting the Reaching Baseball to the Inner-City (RBI) program several years ago. However, I do think that they have somewhat missed a very important part to that program. Currently, if you go to watch an RBI program baseball game, you will often see a team filled with a bunch of black kids or a team filled with a bunch of Hispanic kids playing against another team filled with a bunch of black kids or another team filled with a bunch of Hispanic kids. I realize that one of the major goals of the RBI program is to increase interest in baseball within the inner city and the African American community in general, considering the number of African American players in the Major Leagues is dwindling at an extremely alarming rate. However, the important part of the puzzle that I feel is missing in the RBI program is integration. What are we really teaching our young people by having a team full of black kids play other teams full of black kids while outside the city we have teams full of white kids playing against other teams full of white kids?

How far have we actually come since 1947? We've integrated the Major League, yet we have created our own Negro leagues and segregated white leagues in youth baseball. That doesn't make sense to me. Wouldn't we be doing a much better job of increasing social awareness and well-being if we could somehow get some teams that consisted of four white kids, four African Americans, four Latinos, and four Asian kids? Isn't that what ends up happening at the Major League level anyway? Any Major League roster is a melting pot of ethnic and cultural backgrounds, yet at the grassroots level of youth baseball, we're still as segregated today as we were in the 1940s. The great Martin Luther King Jr. would be ashamed.

What are we really preparing these youngsters for in the long haul if we can't teach them how to socialize with teammates of a different skin tone or from a different cultural background? I have an extremely difficult time believing that with all of the resources that Major League Baseball has at their disposal that they haven't been able to figure out a way to integrate youth baseball in this day and age. Yes, I realize that a black kid can play on a primarily white team and that there are no real rules preventing it as there were in 1947. However, I am pretty sure that if you took a poll in youth baseball today, that you will find that there is still a very real color barrier.

If a player is fortunate enough to move on to play big-time college or professional baseball, that is in most cases the first time that they will really be in a setting where they are in constant contact with players of a different race or cultural background. For many of them, that may be way too late for them to overcome their own prejudices.

In many cases, the color line that is drawn in youth baseball ends up being the color green. Green as in the color of money; many of the top AAU, USSSA, or CABA travel programs out there cost a considerable amount of money to cover their travel costs. Unfortunately, for many kids in an urban setting, white or black, even with fundraising opportunities available, they could never afford to play on one of those types of travel teams. You would think that some way, somehow Major League Baseball could incorporate some sort of grant program into the RBI program that would allow urban kids to participate in some of the more elite traveling programs that are out there. Baseball is losing kids every day to other sports and it all comes down to money. It is much less expensive to play basketball, soccer, track, and many other sports than it is to play baseball. Nowadays, just to play single game can be extremely costly. Once you're done paying for umpires, field rental, and baseballs, you're already close to over $200 just for that one game in some cases.

I can only hope and dream that someday the game of baseball will be integrated at every level from the very top to the very bottom. It's now over sixty years since Jackie Robinson broke the color barrier in the Major League. We're long overdue to get it right everywhere else as well.

CHAPTER 12

The Common Thread Of The Game

One of the greatest things that I can attribute to the game of baseball is the countless memories and friendships that I've made over the years, both playing and coaching. Those are the things that will last a lifetime and beyond.

The funniest thing about that statement is that some of the best memories I have never even took place on the baseball field. They were at a friend's house, at a restaurant after a game, you name it. They were the times when we just sat and talked for hours about nothing and everything all at the same time. The bonds that you build through the game are simply amazing. I've both played and coached on some pretty great baseball teams, yet the best memories are still off the field. That is the one intangible about baseball and any other sport for that matter. The tie that binds is an amazing bond. It is sometimes very difficult to describe and, truthfully, unless the person that you are trying to describe it to is someone who has been a part of a team, you can never really make someone else understand what you are talking about. If you haven't experienced it for yourself, you'll have a hard time understanding what I am trying to explain.

It's kind of like baseball was the catalyst of so much in my life, the one common thread that binds everything else together. I have so much to be thankful for that has been a result of the game, but some of the best things that I can remember aren't necessarily directly involved with the game or what happened on the baseball field, but more so as result of the game.

It's funny when I first started thinking about putting this chapter into the book; I thought it would be very easy to write. As it turned out, this might have been the toughest chapter to write simply because trying to narrow it down to just a few of the great memories that I have from playing and coaching turned out to be a daunting task. There are so many that deserve to be mentioned that trying to pick out just a few was very tough, but I did my best. Some of these were more of a "type of memory" as opposed to the actual incident, but I think that you'll get the point.

One of my best memories is the simple fact of how everything first started in amateur baseball for me. Long before a pitch was ever thrown by someone wearing a Berkshire Baseball uniform, the game itself already started making some memories for me. Back when I first got involved in amateur baseball in 1989, I was literally just a kid myself. I was two years out of high school and I had played one summer of slow-pitch softball because, in our area, that was really the closest thing to organized baseball that we had at the time. While I had a lot of fun playing slow-pitch softball that summer, I also realized that slow-pitch softball and "real" baseball were two drastically different games. At the end of the season, I vowed that unless I was at a family reunion, I would not be playing slow-pitch softball again anytime soon.

At the time, I was working for a company called Meridian Asset Management, which for lack of a better term, was the trust department of Meridian Bank. My boss at the time, Russ Herbein was, like myself, a huge baseball fan. Throughout the summer, I would make comments to him about how much I really didn't like playing slow-pitch softball and how different it was from baseball. I guess I was just venting at the time, but after the season ended, we were talking over lunch about it again, and I basically came out and said we should probably just start an adult baseball league.

Russ is twenty-two years older than I am, so he was forty-two and I was only twenty years old when I came up with this idea. Just a few months prior to that, he had convinced me to join his Optimist Club. So as we were talking about this, he had actually come up with the idea of starting the league with the Spring-Lawn Optimist Club as the sponsor of the league. Frankly, I was just looking for a way to keep from playing softball ever again, so I was up to listening to any idea that would help me achieve that goal.

So at our next Optimist Club meeting, we presented the idea to the club and they agreed to move forward with it. Russ knew Al Nerino, one of the bigwigs at our local newspaper, the *Reading Eagle Company* at the time, so he called him to set up a meeting so that we could get some publicity about the idea. As it turned out, Al was a huge "baseball guy" himself and was completely sold on the idea. Right off the bat he started talking about his playing days and a league that he had played in as an amateur in the Allentown, Pennsylvania area and went on and on about old baseball stories. He was so pumped up about the idea that he got the sports editor, Mike Zielinski, into his office and started telling him how the story would be laid out and I was just sitting there at the age of twenty, thinking to myself, "Wow, this is really going to happen." Al and Mike decided that a reporter by the name of Dave Kutch would do the article and everything just took off from there. The meeting lasted for about an hour, which actually made Russ and me late getting back from lunch, but Russ was the boss, so we didn't really get into any trouble.

After that meeting, as the remainder of the day went on, I still remember thinking, even though I was only a young man, about how powerful the game of baseball was. I mean here Russ and me, some twenty years apart in age and the editor and sports editor of the county's largest paper had just sat for over an hour telling each other old baseball stories. Actually, I didn't really tell any old stories, I just sat and listened the whole time, just taking it all in, thinking that someday, I wanted to be the guy telling these great stories. The common thread was baseball. Right off the bat, no pun intended, a few strangers sat and talked as though they had been friends for years and it was all because of baseball. Tough to explain, but I've seen it happen thousands of times.

It makes me think of James Earl Jones as he was playing Terence Mann in the movie *Field of Dreams* and explaining to Kevin Costner's character, Ray Kinsella that he must keep his baseball field simply because the game of baseball can put a grip on you that you cannot explain.

It is by far one of the best quotes in movie history, I refer to it often, and every time I watch the movie, my eyes will start to tear up during this part. I would be doing myself an injustice if I had written a book and didn't include this quote in it because it has had a huge influence on everything that I do in regard to the game of baseball.

"People will come, Ray. They'll come to Iowa for reasons they can't even fathom. They'll turn up your driveway not knowing for sure why they're doing it. They'll arrive at your door as innocent as children, longing for the past. Of course, we won't mind if you look around, you'll say. It's only $20 per person. They'll pass over the money without even thinking about it: for it is money they have and peace they lack. And they'll walk out to the bleachers; sit in shirtsleeves on a perfect afternoon. They'll find they have reserved seats somewhere along one of the baselines, where they sat when they were children and cheered their heroes. And they'll watch the game and it'll be as if they dipped themselves in magic waters. The memories will be so thick they'll have to brush them away from their faces. People will come, Ray. The one constant through all the years, Ray, has been baseball. America has rolled by like an army of steamrollers. It has been erased like a blackboard, rebuilt and erased again. But baseball has marked the time. This field, this game: it's a part of our past, Ray. It reminds of us of all that once was good and it could be again. Oh... people will come, Ray. People will most definitely come.

~ James Earl Jones as Terence Mann
*From the movie **Field of Dreams***

If you read that over and over as I have, it is a very powerful statement. As I have stated several times before in this book, baseball has always acted as a type of sanctuary for me. That day, in the offices of the *Reading Eagle Company*, that was so evident to me. To see the editor and sports editor simply forget about all of the hustle and bustle of running a newspaper for over an hour just to talk about the game of baseball proves how powerful the grip of the game can be on you.

As it turned out, the *Reading Eagle* ran the article on October 15, 1989, and we had the organizational meeting for the Spring-Lawn Optimist Baseball League at the Sinking Spring Fire Company on October 17, 1989, the same day that the World Series was halted due to an earthquake in the Bay Area. That night marked the formation of both the Spring-Lawn Optimist Baseball League and the Berkshire Red Sox Baseball Club, which later became the Berkshire Baseball & Softball Club. I can certainly say that from that night on, my life has never been the same.

The day after the meeting, as various other media outlets started contacting Russ and me regarding the formation of the league, Russ spun his chair around and said to me, "Do you have any idea what we just did?"

I simply replied, "What do you mean?"

"We're in the process of changing amateur baseball history here in Berks County," he said.

I thought for a second and just smiled and said, "Cool."

Although, I'm not really sure now, at that time I really did understand what was happening and with hindsight being twenty-twenty, my simple ignorance of the fact that twenty-year-old kids shouldn't start organizations like this was more than likely my biggest asset at the time.

That first year, I coached guys who I had graduated high school with two years prior or played against in high school, not to mention guys who were several years older than I was. Now that was a daunting task. It really wasn't something that I wanted to do at the time, I really just wanted to play baseball, but somebody had to coach us. So that was how I got my start in coaching. Coaching guys my age and guys much older, and somehow we made it work out. We went 18-3 in our league and 24-8 overall, losing a gut-wrenching League Championship Series three games to two to a team that we had beaten seven out of seven times in the regular season. I wasn't the type of "player/manager" that would put myself in the lineup every day; on the days when I did put myself in the lineup, I would bat myself lower in the order. I think that philosophy went a long way in getting my players, who were also my peers, to respond to me and to respect me. As I said earlier, respect is earned and I think I earned a lot of respect from those guys when they saw that I was willing to put the team's wants and needs ahead of my own.

During our league opener in 1989, I had to set the tone to prove to my players that I was going to be fair. Our league opened up the season, with every team in the league playing a doubleheader against two separate teams; we called it the "Opening Day Jamboree." All the teams in the league played at the same location, Twin Valley High School. We were trying to make it a big deal and promote the start of the league in a big way. When I announced the lineup for the first game, I wasn't in it. I know for a fact that immediately, with that move alone, I earned a lot of guys' respect.

In game two, I started myself behind the plate, batted myself in the eighth spot in the order, and ended up going 3-for-4 with a three-run home run and five RBIs. The dinger was the first in our organization's history, by the way, and trailing at the time, it put us ahead to stay and helped us complete our opening day sweep.

The following Wednesday for our next game, I again was not in the starting lineup and again proved to my players and teammates that I was willing to make the tough decisions and put the team's needs ahead of my own wants.

To be honest, if you remember the whole idea of starting an amateur baseball team and league was so that *I could play baseball*, not coach it. I wanted to play every day; that was the whole point. I didn't want to coach at all, but I guess sometimes you find your calling in life in different ways.

So the memories started to pile up quickly, the players became friends and the bonds started to seal for what would last a lifetime. Many of the guys who I played with or coached have moved on. Life has taken over and baseball has taken a backseat for many of them. Even after several years though, the minute you run into them somewhere, the memories seem to overtake you like a tidal wave. My wife sometimes makes fun of me because she always tells me that we can't go anywhere without running into someone that I know and, yes, I usually know them through baseball. We've run into people that I know from baseball in restaurants, grocery stores, Clearwater, Florida, at Phillies Spring Training games, a Journey concert, you name it and we've run into someone that I know through baseball. Every time that it happens, we'll stand and talk about some old memories on the field or off, and then once we head our separate ways, I'll look at my wife and she'll smile and say something to the effect of "unbelievable," and we'll both just laugh. In all honesty, though, those times are the times that I may cherish even more than the times on the field itself. That's when you realize what a large part the game has played in your life, and you understand that it is more the thread than the fabric.

It always amazes me how complete strangers can find the game of baseball as such a common bond; it's exactly what James Earl Jones talks about in that quote from *Field of Dreams*. It's like when people even just start talking about the game of baseball; they can forget about everything else that is going on in their lives.

I once heard someone say that if you could have just sat George W. Bush and Fidel Castro down together in a room and have them start a conversation about baseball, you would be amazed at how the political differences would have quickly been forgotten. It is something that is beyond me when it comes to trying to understand the bond that the game has on people from all walks of life. How it brings back memories of childhood and better times. It is truly fascinating to me.

I remember one time when I had gone to a Harrisburg Senators game on City Island with two friends of mine, Tod Whitman and Eric Sanders. Tod, who we would sometimes refer to as Tod with one "D," had played for us for a few years. He had moved from Reading to Harrisburg and we just stayed in touch after he moved. This was just one of those nights when we figured we'd get together to catch up and what better spot to do it at then at a Minor League baseball game. I was working with Eric and he was simply a complete sports freak, so anytime I would ever suggest going anywhere that involved baseball or any other sport, Eric was certainly up for the trip. After the game, we were just standing outside of the stadium talking about the "good ole days" when Tod played for us. Eric and Tod had only met each other that night and I'm sure that they've never seen each other since, so the bond of baseball started to work its magic again on this particular evening. There was a set of batting cages along the Susquehanna River and as we were standing there their chatting, we were also watching a gentleman who was probably in his fifties hitting in the cage, making various observations, and just talking about baseball.

After the gentleman who was taking his batting practice finished up, I'm not sure how or why anymore, but he came up to us and joined in our conversation about baseball. Again, this was amazing, the four of us stood there and just talked about baseball literally for hours. The cages and rides that surrounded the stadium on City Island all slowly started to close and the lights turned off and we just stood there by a streetlight talking about baseball. As if none of us had anything else to do in the world. We had been dipped into that magic water that James Earl Jones referred to in that quote, and none of us had a care in the world. We stood there and talked until two o'clock in the morning before Tod looked at his watch and said, "Holy crap, it is 2:00 a.m.; Cindy's going to kill me."

I agreed that my wife would not be happy either and we all scampered off into the night like a bunch of little boys who were late for dinner.

As Eric and I made the hour long drive back to Reading, we just kept talking about how bizarre it was that we just stood there in the dark until two o'clock in the morning talking to a complete stranger about nothing other than baseball.

Amazingly enough, about two years or so after that night, I ran into that same gentleman, whose name I still can't remember, at a place in Perry County called *Double Day Country Inn and Farm*. A man had built a baseball field in a cornfield on his farm, similar to the field in *Field of Dreams*, and turned his farmhouse into a bed and breakfast. He would then bring retired big leaguers in and charge participants to play games with them while wearing old-fashioned wool baseball uniforms. It was actually a pretty ingenious idea. I had gone there, played in games with Tug McGraw, Al Oliver, and John Kruk, and had a blast every single time. On this particular day, I was amazed to run into my "old friend" and we again reminisced about old baseball stories and that night by the river. I think we talked for about another two or three hours. I haven't seen him since that day at the farm, but I'm sure if I ever run into him again, we'll talk for a few hours.

Those types of "stories" make the game so precious to me, I love to hear them and I love to tell them. Again, it's that magical common bond that only the game of baseball can provide.

We had played in a tournament in 1993 in Berwick, Pennsylvania, the Tri-County Invitational. The same North Berwick team that had beaten us in the championship game of the Unionville Tournament where the little racial incident occurred the year before invited us. A patriarch of the game, named Al Steward Sr., managed the North Berwick club. He was so impressed with the way that we had conducted ourselves at the Unionville event that he was convinced that our organization was the class of amateur baseball in the area, and that he had to have us come up and play in their tournament.

It was a sixteen-team single-elimination event and the way the brackets were drawn up, we opened up the tournament in the final game of the day against one of the Tri-County League's top teams, the Auferio's A's. Due to Al Steward telling every other team in the tournament as well as the local paper, that we were the team to beat going into the weekend, we had quite a large target on our backs. When we saw copies of the newspaper article hanging on the wall of our opponents' dugout, we knew we'd have to play good baseball all weekend to keep up with the hype. The role of the underdog is so much easier to live up to because you have nothing to lose.

The article mentioned how we had a former Philadelphia Phillies farmhand named Rick Dunnum as our ace pitcher and that we were coached by a gentleman named Del Mintz or had been drafted out of high school by the Detroit Tigers, so everyone was gunning for us. The problem was that we left Reading that weekend with Rick on his way to Maryland to attend a country music festival and the only way we'd see him on the mound was if we would advance to the semifinals Sunday afternoon.

We stumbled right out of the gate and trailed the Auferio's the entire game. As we approached the final innings, one of the local clubs, Orloski's, had already played their first two rounds of games and advanced into the semifinals on Sunday before we had even completed our first game. They decided to stop by and see what all of the hype about the Berkshire Red Sox was really all about. They relished in seeing us trailing and, in the back of a pickup truck with a few adult beverages, they became more and more obnoxious as the innings got shorter.

We were trailing 6-5 entering the top of the seventh inning and our first two hitters were each quietly retired. This really seemed to make the Orloski's players overjoyed and more vocal than ever. Our next batter, Tom Hankey, slapped a single up the middle to give us a little spark, but certainly not enough to quiet the peanut gallery that had assembled along the third base line. Our next hitter was a guy named Mike Stern, who was a left-handed first baseman with a striking resemblance to Babe Ruth. Our new classy friends from Orloski's, however, felt that he resembled the "Michelin Man" more than the "the Great Bambino" and had no problem with letting Mike know. After three pitches and two absolutely horrendous swings, Mike found himself quickly in the hole with a 1-and-2 count. Mike connected with the next pitch, however, and hit it off the roof of the house that sat about fifty feet beyond the right field fence to give us a 7-6 lead. Mike quietly trotted around the bases and tipped his helmet to his new fan club as he rounded third base. We held them in the bottom of the seventh and advanced to the quarterfinals on Sunday.

Our quarterfinal game on Sunday against Honey Pot got off to the same start as our opening round game did the day before. We trailed 8-2 after three and a half innings and it again looked as though we would not be able to live up to the hype that was created before we got there.

Staying focused, we just kept chipping away until we again found ourselves trailing by a run entering the bottom of the seventh inning with one out, and we had runners on second and third when Erron Archie stepped to the plate. Erron smoked a single to left to tie the game and when the Honey Pot leftfielder bobbled the ball, it allowed Mike Stern to score the winning run and catapult us into the semifinals. This was an extra good comeback for us, considering our ace pitcher, Rick Dunnum, was in the process of making a four-hour drive from Maryland to Berwick to pitch for us in the semifinals. There weren't too many guys who were excited about the prospect of telling Rick that he had made that drive for nothing, so the comeback was that much sweeter.

In the semifinals, Rick was lights out, after yielding a run in the top of the first inning to put us behind, which was probably more due to a four-hour drive than anything else. He cruised the rest of the way. We won 7-2 in a rather uneventful game compared to our previous two. Rick tossed sixty-eight pitches in a complete game effort. However, our back-up catcher pulled a hamstring in the semifinal game, which on the surface doesn't sound like a big deal until you realize that our scheduled championship game pitcher was our *starting* catcher. Without a third catcher on the trip and our pitching staff depleted, things did not look good for us as we were looking at facing the State College Merchants in the title game. State College had spanked us two weeks earlier in our own Rawlings Berkshire Showdown tournament 9-0 and they had one-hit us in the process. As Del and I tried to figure out what we were going to do, Rick came up to us and said, "I'll start. Let's get it going now while I'm still warm."

At first, Del and I were not thrilled with the idea, but Rick insisted that he was a former pro; he knew what he was doing and was going to take the ball. We reluctantly agreed and Rick took the hill for his second straight start.

State College quickly jumped out to a 4-0 lead in the top of the first inning and made our decision to start Rick look like the biggest bone-head move in baseball history. However, in the bottom of the second, we went out and put our own "four spot" on the board to tie the game.

Rick helped himself out in the bottom of the fifth inning with an RBI double to put us up 5-4. As we had all weekend, we were not going to make this game easy either. State College had runners on first and second with two outs in the bottom of the seventh inning and their catcher, Chris Frank, was at the plate. Frank hit a line-drive bullet down the third base line that off the bat looked like it would at least tie the game, if not win it. However, our player/manager, Del Mintz, who was playing third base at the time, made an incredible diving catch to end the game and give us our first tournament title in the organization's history.

It was truly an incredible weekend. Everyone on the squad pitched in and helped out. Rick Dunnum and Erron Archie were named co-MVPs for the weekend, but it was truly a team effort to take home that title.

The best part of the story actually took place seven years later when our 18-U team was playing the Moosic Mets in a doubleheader just outside of Scranton, Pennsylvania. Between games, I was talking to the umpire, exchanging pleasantries, when he took a trip down memory lane that made my jaw drop.

He said, "You know the best game I ever umpired involved another team called the Red Sox as well and I think they might have been from the Reading area too.

"It was at the Tri-County Invitational tournament down in Berwick," he continued. "They had a guy who had played minor league ball who started in both the semifinal and championship games on the mound in the tournament. Even more amazing, the guy threw back-to-back complete games and won them both!

"Man, that guy never threw a pitch down the middle of the plate!" he exclaimed.

As I told him that I remembered that weekend quite vividly myself, we both just laughed and were kind of amazed at what a small world we live in. Again, this is just one of those things that amaze me about the game of baseball. Even at just the amateur level, one simple little weekend when everything just fell into place made a huge impact on not only our team, but several other people as well. That's the stuff that memories are made of.

Over the years, my wife and I have been invited to some of my current and former players' graduation parties and weddings. We've shared births and unfortunately a few funerals already as well. Those are all the times when you get to sit and reflect on what it all means and how much of an influence you may have had on someone's life, again, those are the memories that will always mean the most to me. It is a great honor to be invited to a function such as a graduation or wedding. You realize that you have made an impact on that player's life, he actually regards you as part of his family, and that is incredible.

As a coach, many times players will confide in you even more than they will confide in their own parents. I'm not sure why that is, but it happens very often. I think sometimes they look at you as an adult figure they can confide in, a parent-type figure, but a friend as well. I've had players call me because they were arguing with their girlfriend, struggling during their high school season, considering transferring schools, parents are getting divorced, you name it and I have probably received a phone call about it at some point in my life. Those again are the memories that outweigh the "X's and O's" of coaching baseball. That a young man has enough confidence in you to talk to you about his problems is rewarding and can always help to put things into perspective if you ever start to lose sight of why we are really here anyway.

Obviously, over the course of twenty-plus years of coaching baseball, I have coached quite a few players. Clearly to stay in touch with every one of them would be impossible. Although, I truly wish that I could. Our organization holds an annual banquet and I always love nothing more than when former players come back to the banquet just to get reacquainted and to say hi. As a coach and the guy who runs the organization, that is extremely rewarding to me.

I try to keep in touch with as many of my former players as I can, but again, the sheer numbers make that an extremely daunting task.

Our organization was recently in Charlotte, North Carolina, to play in a tournament. Right before we were getting ready to leave, I remembered seeing on *Facebook* that one of my former players, Nick Allen, was now living in Charlotte. I quickly shot him an e-mail and message on *Facebook* to see if we could get together. Fortunately, even on short notice, we were able to get together for lunch one day.

This kind of thing helps you realize why you coach. We had a great lunch catching up on old times and simply talking baseball. Nick had gone on to play at Villanova for four years and then was drafted by the Seattle Mariners and played three years in the Mariners organization before being released. He was great kid and it made me proud of him to see how well he was doing.

After lunch, I got to thinking about that lunch and about the relationship that Nick and I had. The funniest thing is the simple fact that I actually coached Nick for only four games in his life. The other games that he played in our organization, he actually played for a different coach. I again realized how much of an impact you can have on a person's life in a very short time. Coaching a kid for four games over one weekend tournament ten years earlier forged a great relationship. For whatever reason we just stayed in touch, I would go down to see him play at Villanova occasionally. Unfortunately, with him playing in the Mariners system, I never had the opportunity to see him play professionally.

Some of my favorite memories include making that drive down to Villanova to see two of my former players pitch against each other when Villanova, with Nick Allen on the mound, would face off against the University of Pittsburgh, with Nick Evangelista on the mound. I always wondered what the chances were of two players that played together facing each other at the Division I college level, and here tiny little Berkshire Baseball had two guys doing it for three years straight. Evangelista was a year ahead of Allen.

Those truly are the times in my life when I realize how fortunate I am to coach as many quality young men as I have. The stuff that happens on the field is always great, but those lunches, trips to a college to see them play, and just talking on the phone or exchanging e-mails long after they are no longer playing for you really make you see the big picture.

One thing that I can say with certainty is that every player that I have ever coached has and always will hold a special place in my heart, even those who I would occasionally clash with; they were all special.

I've learned so much from every one of them. I can only hope that they learned half as much from me.

CHAPTER 13

The Memories Of The Game

*T*his is another incredibly difficult chapter for me to write because coaching and playing the game of baseball have created a vast number of memories for me. Where can I possibly start?

Although my involvement as a coach with the game of baseball has always been at the youth and amateur levels, the game has certainly allowed me to log some serious miles over the years.

From the very beginning, we traveled. We started out on some short trips, keeping us with in the state of Pennsylvania. We embarked to places like Harrisburg, State College, Williamsport, and Berwick to play in tournaments in the early 1990s. We slowly started to go farther, adding New York, New Jersey, Maryland, Virginia, and Delaware to the list of stops along the way. With every new place that we traveled to, we met new friends and rivals, all the while adding to the memories.

Once we branched into the youth baseball ranks, we really started logging some serious miles. Making stops in East Cobb, Georgia; Orlando, Florida; Galveston, Texas; Las Vegas, Nevada; Myrtle Beach, South Carolina; Wheeling, West Virginia; Charlotte, North Carolina; and

Cocoa Beach, Florida, to just name a few. Again each stop added some new memories.

Whether it was an entire season, a weekend tournament, or just a single game, some of the memories just seem to be embedded in my mind. I'm going to try to pick a few out here to share with you, but I will be leaving so many out that its almost like this entire chapter may be doing an injustice, but I'll give it a shot and try not to bore you too much with it.

I guess it is only fitting to start with the first team that I ever coached. As I said earlier in the book, this first team back in 1990 was comprised of guys that I had played with and against in high school and several players that were considerably younger. Again, I coached this team more out of necessity than desire. I can't say that while growing up, my dream was to be a baseball coach but this was the first step in the direction of being able to achieve that dream. My dream was to play professional baseball, I realized that wasn't going to happen somewhere around my junior year of high school. So the formation of the Berkshire Red Sox and the Spring-Lawn Optimist Baseball League was again to allow me to continue to *play* baseball, not something to be fulfilling of my desire to *coach* baseball.

As the season approached and it became more and more evident that I would be the first player/manager in the history of our organization, I had begun to reluctantly accept the role and then determined that if I was going to do it, I was going to do it right, not half-assed. As I said earlier, gaining the respect of my teammates and players was a huge concern for me. If I approached it with my wants and desires to play every day being more important than the needs of the team, that first season would have been disastrous and the coaching career that I really didn't want would have ended ugly, very quickly.

We had a very good team that year, our pitching was awesome, our hitters were dangerous, we had team speed, and most importantly, we had great chemistry. We went 18-3 in the regular season, 24-8 overall and ended up losing in our league championship series three games to two. Still one of the most painful losses I've ever experienced as both a coach and a player. We were so much better than the team that we played in our League Championship Series; we had beaten them seven out of seven times in the regular season and ended up losing to them three games to two in the League Championship Series.

Although we didn't accomplish our ultimate goal that year, that team was extremely special to me as a coach. I guess that you could say that they were kind of like your first love or your first kiss; you'll never forget them. We had a great group of guys who were truly pioneers for our organization, even though we had no idea that we were pioneers at the time. We were all so young at the time that if you had ever asked any of us if we would have thought that the organization would grow to sponsor over twenty teams and be looking at celebrating our twenty-fifth anniversary in 2014, I am sure that we all would have just laughed. The one thing we realized at that time was that we wanted to do things the right way and for the right reasons. We wanted to hustle on and off the field, we wanted to look good as a team, and we wanted to be the best. Right out of the gate, we wanted to set a very high standard, raise the bar; so to speak, so that people could notice that we were different. We didn't want to be just another team, another organization out there playing baseball. So right from the start, without even realizing it, we established our "Tradition of Excellence" motto that our organization now holds very dear to their hearts. Today we try to make the kids in the organization realize what they are a part of. That very first team, as I said, had great chemistry. We were friends first and teammates second. We hung out together; we ended up attending each other's weddings, kid's birthdays, and unfortunately even one funeral so far.

Shortly after we got started, in our third season in 1992, I received a phone call from the recreation director at Graterford Prison, a maximum security prison just outside of Philadelphia. This phone call was long before the Internet and our Web site, so I'm still not sure how he found out about us, but he did. The phone call consisted of some small talk about our organization and one very important question: would we be interested in coming to the prison and playing a team of inmates that called themselves the Graterford Pirates? Without hesitation, I said yes.

We set the date and put the game on our schedule.

When we arrived at the prison, we had to go through a very intense security screening. We were not allowed to bring in any money or tobacco, the only metal that we could have were our bats at that time and what was on our cleats. We went through security in groups of two. Del Mintz, who was actually our head coach at the time and I, who was now just an assistant, were the first ones through security. After we cleared security, we had to wait in another holding area as the rest of the team cleared security. As Del and I stood there waiting for everyone else, we were looking along a wall full of photographs of prison guards. At first look, Del said to me, "So what do you think this is? Are these guys like the employee of the month or something?"

He then paused and looked a little closer at the print under each photo, and said, "Holy crap, these are all guys who have been killed in the line of duty here!"

"What the @%*# have you gotten us into?" he asked me.

"They were looking for a game," I said.

Once everyone made their way through security, we had to walk down to the "yard" in a double line, as if we were back in grade school, only this time we were flanked by eight guards carrying shotguns. As we got into the yard and approached the field, we may have been a bit intimidated. I can't honestly say that I knew what to expect when I agreed to play this game. I certainly was not aware that not only were we playing a team that was made up of convicted felons and the game would be umpired by convicted felons, but we would also be playing in front of about three thousand "fans," who were all convicted felons as well. I think we were all a little bit in awe at this point.

We got loose and started the game. We jumped out to an early lead in the first inning and then when we took the field in the bottom of the first, we gave the inmates a special treat when we trotted our ace pitcher and former professional, Rick Dunnum out to the mound. Rick had his best stuff that day and the fans quickly realized that we were pretty good. The crowd of over a thousand inmates, I guess you could call them a captive audience, started rooting for us right then and there. They jeered at everything that the Pirates did and were wowed by Rick on the mound and Erron Archie at the plate, who just happened to hit a mammoth home run off of the cell block that was well over four-hundred feet away from home plate in his second at-bat and quickly became a fan favorite.

After four innings, the inmates had yet to record a hit off Rick and we were already up on them 8-0. We pulled Rick out of the game and pitched by committee the rest of the way en route to an 18-6 victory.

The fans had to all exit in the seventh inning because it was mealtime and their time out in the yard was over for the day.

After the game, as we were shaking hands with the inmates, they were all incredibly grateful that we were willing to make the trip. They greeted us with smiles even though we had just beaten them by twelve runs. They complimented us on how we played the game and told us that we were a very good team with a lot of class. I think the fact that we "called the dogs off" early in the game did a lot for how they reacted to us. We literally could have scored another ten runs that day and had we not pulled Rick out of the game after the fourth inning, they may have felt differently about that. Once we realized that we were considerably better than they were that day, we didn't do anything differently than we would have if we were not playing a team of convicted felons. We stopped stealing, we went station to station if it was possible, and we beat them with a lot of class.

Out of all of things that happened that day, what I remember most was how grateful they were for us just showing up. Their coach had told me right from the start that they would literally ask hundreds of teams every summer to come play them and if they could get eight to ten games a year scheduled, they were fortunate. It was another one of those times where baseball served as a great healer. For those three-plus hours that we played those guys, they were not thieves, rapists, and murderers; they were all just baseball players. Men acting like kids, playing a game in the hot sun and cherishing every minute of it. It really didn't matter to them that their own "hometown fans" started rooting for the visitors in the first inning. It really didn't matter to them that they lost 18-6. It really didn't matter to them that that they were no-hit for the first four innings by a former professional pitcher. The only thing that mattered to those guys on that day was that they were playing baseball, and they loved every minute of it.

The summer of 2006 was an extremely memorable and rewarding season for me as a coach. The collegiate age Berkshire Red Sox team that I coached had to overcome a great deal of adversity in order to capture our second championship in four years.

It certainly wasn't an easy task, in mid-June; it looked as though our teams' run of three straight trips to the league championship series was in serious jeopardy.

The club was 3-5 in league play, 22-19 overall and had just dropped three games in a row in our own Rawlings Berkshire Showdown tournament, which they were looking to defend the title to.

Our pitching staff and defense, which were supposed to be our strong suits had just given up 44 runs in their last six games and things looked pretty bleak.

The team called a players only meeting and to a man determined that they would turn the season around. We went 17-1-1 in our final 19 league games and finished one point behind the Lititz Pirates for the regular season title. The second place finish earned us a bye in the first round of the play-offs, where we faced a familiar foe, Smitty's Cardinals, in a very unfamiliar setting.

The Cardinals and our club had met in the League Championship Series in the previous three seasons. 2003 went to us and the Cardinals had swept us in both 2004 and 2005, three-games-to-none.

It looked to be the same old post-season story as the precious two years when we met up in the best-of-five game semi-final series when the Cards jumped out to a commanding two-games-to-none lead with a 5-0 win in game one and an 8-4 victory in game two.

Heading to Lancaster for games three and hopefully four against a team that had owned us in our last eight post-season meetings didn't leave too many people believing that the series would ever return to our home, George Field that Saturday night. Game three didn't show much promise when the Cardinals jumped on our hard throwing lefty, Joe Harris for four two-out runs in the bottom of the first inning.

We answered back with three runs in the top of the second and battled back and forth with the Cards all night before walking away with an 8-6 win and earning the chance to play another day. That evening, a Friday night, we jumped out to a 3-0 lead in the top of the first inning and then were shut down by Cardinals hurler, Dan Myers as he retired 12 of the next 13 batters he faced from the second to the fifth inning.

Smitty's scored a run in the fifth to make it 3-1 and then tied the game in the bottom of the sixth at 3-3.

We got the lead-off man on in the top of the seventh and then bunted into a double-play to kill a would be rally.

Nate Reed, our game one starter entered the game to pitch in the bottom of the seventh.

Reed started the inning by walking Carlos Diaz who was then bunted over to second. We then intentionally walked the Cardinals clean-up hitter Drew Pare to set up the force.

Reed struck out Ryan Sutter for the second out of the inning. We then intentionally walked Brandon Hostetter to face Sean Killian. Killian worked the count full before hitting a rocket up the middle that ricocheted off of Reed's thigh and into Kyle Stover's glove at third, who threw Killian out at first for the final out of the inning, sending the game into extra frames.

Stover then led off the eighth with a single, we again failed to execute a bunt with no outs, but Stover did advance to second on Pete Jordan's walk and then scored on Chad Denunzio's single to give us a 4-3 lead.

Reed took the hill again in the bottom of the eighth inning. He walked the lead-off man and then got a double play ball before striking out Jose Ochoa to end the game and send the series back to Reading tied at two games each.

We sent Jeremy Hess to the mound in game five. Hess was pitching with a heavy heart that night as he had learned earlier in the day that one of his good friends was killed in a car accident the night before.

The Cardinals jumped out to a 2-0 lead in the fourth inning and Andrew Pry was tossing a no-hitter going into the bottom of the fifth for Smitty's.

Denunzio led off the fifth with a single to break up the no-no and we exploded for five runs to go up 5-2. Hess shut down the Cards with a 1-2-3 sixth and looked like a man on a mission.

He got Brett Rhoads to line-out to start the seventh, then walked Dan Myers and hit Brandon Hostetter with a 0-2 pitch to put runners on first and second with one out.

Pare struck-out for the second out of the inning and Ryan Sutter hit a bleeder to load the bases for Carlos Diaz.

Diaz worked a 2-2 count before flying out to Aaron Bertoldi in left field to end the game and seal an improbable comeback.

Jeremy Hess and I hugged during the celebration and Jeremy simply said, "He was out there with me tonight DC, he carried me." It was one of those unforgettable moments that a player and coach get to share.

There was no rest for the weary as we opened up the Quad County Optimist League Championship Series with the Lititz Pirates the very next night at Stumpf Field in Lancaster.

We sent Kevin Walbert to the mound, who had not pitched for the majority of the season due to an arm injury.

Walbert battled all night, but our offense could only muster a single run in the first inning and dropped the series opener 6-1 to fall behind in the best-of-five game series one game to none.

The next night, our offense seemed to be a bit more rejuvenated. Even with Lititz sending their ace, Mark Brown to the mound, the Sox scored two runs in the first inning and another four in the third inning off of a Chad Denunzio (2-for-2, 5 RBI) grand slam to take a 6-0 lead.

Brown completed the inning and made way for Matt Gale, Aaron Bertoldi quickly greeted Gale with an inside the park home run in the fourth and we added another four runs in the fifth inning to go up 11-0.

Lititz spoiled Kevin Lengyel's shut-out with a run in the bottom of the seventh, but we knotted the series at a game a piece heading back home to George Field for games three and four.

Lefty Joe Harris took the hill for us and struggled a bit early again, yielding three runs in the first two innings.

Our offense looked sluggish as Bobby Thompson baffled us for four innings, yielding only two hits. In the bottom of the fifth inning, Thompson began to tire and we strung together four singles, but could only plate one run to close the gap to 3-1.

Harris stayed in his groove, by tossing another shut-out inning in the sixth and keeping the Pirates lead at 3-1.

With a full moon rising up over the Pagoda in the distance at George field, Lititz brought in closer Jarred Ellis (1-0, 3 saves, 1.29 ERA), who had been lights out all season long to face the heart of our order.

Ellis had some uncharacteristic control problems as Pete Jordan and Chad Denunzio each led off the inning with walks. That made way for Zac Schneider, who sacrificed both into scoring position and Rob Lozenski's two RBI single tied the game at three.

We couldn't take the lead and hoped that Harris could continue to cruise and keep the game tied.

Lititz had a different idea and scored a run in the top of the seventh to take a 4-3 lead.

With Ellis still on the mound for Lititz, we had Kyle Stover leading off in the bottom of the seventh. He drew a walk and Leon Adams reached on an error to put runners on second and third with no outs with our clean-up hitter, Pete Jordan coming to the plate.

Jordan battled Ellis before finally striking-out on an eight pitch at-bat. Lititz then intentionally walked Chad Denunzio to load the bases.

Zac Schneider struck-out for the second out of the inning, making pinch-hitter Kevin Lengyel the final hope for us.

Lengyel fell behind in the count 1-2 before hitting a single between second and third that scored both Stover and Adams to win the game and take a two-games-to-one series lead.

We had been using the championship season of 2003 as a rally cry since falling behind two-games-to-none in the semi-finals against Smitty's and we had become quite superstitious during that play-off run.

The guys felt that August 9, 2006 would bring the same magic to us as August 6, 2003 had.

August 6, 2003 was the date of game 4 of the 2003 Quad County LCS, a game that was also played on a Wednesday night at George Field.

That night in 2003, we had worn our pinstripe pants and blue jersey's, we would do the same on this night as well. That night in 2003, we had sent Nick Evangelista, who was then attending the University of Pittsburgh and was drafted by the Philadelphia Phillies to the mound. This night we would send Nate Reed, who was also attending the University of Pittsburgh and was being courted by the Philadelphia Phillies earlier that summer, to the mound.

I guess that you could say that the baseball gods were smiling and everything seemed to be right as the we were determined to not go back to Lancaster for game five.

We scored two runs in the bottom of the first inning to jump out to a 2-0 lead.

Reed struggled early, throwing 40 pitches in the first two innings but in spite of sending 10 hitters to the plate, the Pirates could only scratch out one run.

We added three runs in the third inning and another two in the fourth to take a commanding 7-1 lead.

Reed (6 IP, 1 H, 10 K, 4 BB) had settled in, retiring 12 of the next thirteen batters that he faced from the third to the sixth inning.

Matt Zaorski, Nick Zerbe and Kevin Morganti combined to throw a scoreless seventh inning and secure our third title in franchise history and our first since 2003.

An incredible three day celebration was kicked off that night, which included fireworks in the outfield and champagne in the locker room.

These guys were bridesmaids no more, after two runner-up finishes in a row; they finally got the monkey off of their backs.

Some of the same players from the 2006 team were also on the 2003 championship team and that was great, it was the first league championship team that I had ever managed, so that will always be a special group to me.

The 2006 team, however, they were something else, we were 3-5 in the league at one point, we were down two games-to-none to Smitty's in that semifinal series and the core of that group of kids were on the teams that came up short in the previous two seasons. That was what really proved their resilience, the rookies on that club rose to the occasion and the veterans led the way, as far as chemistry goes, that group had something special, and it was the perfect storm. I think that every member of that team will remember that season for a long time to come. I know that I will.

That 2006 Berkshire Red Sox team made history, winning the title and finishing 46-25-1 overall.

I'm not sure that anyone would have thought that we'd repeat in 2007, but this core group of players perhaps made that five year stretch from 2003 through 2007 some of my best years as a coach. So when the 2007 season started, we had quite a target on our back.

After making four straight trips to the League Championship Series and bringing home the titles in both 2003 and 2006, we knew that we would have to play some real good baseball in 2007 to maintain that "Tradition of Excellence".

The season started with a solid core of returning players and as always, we had also added some new faces.

Rookies, Shane Stein, Nate Weiss, Gerry Werner, Eric Hetrich and Carlos Benitez, who had just defected from Cuba, were all looking to help keep us on top.

Josh McDevitt, who was a legion double-roster player, was hoping to pitch in for us on legion off days.

We added Dan Myers, who had played for Smitty's for the previous few years to add some versatility and veteran leadership to the squad.

Early season losses of pitchers, Kevin Lengyel and Kevin Walbert as well as another season ending concussion for John Pisker left us with some holes to fill.

We opened our season with a decisive 8-1 road victory over the Lititz Pirates in a rematch of the 2006 LCS and looked to be running on all cylinders to start.

As good as we looked in that league opener; we looked that bad in our next game as we dropped a 4-3 loss to the SWS Nationals in the final inning.

For the better part of the season, that was the story of this group, one night they would look unstoppable and the next night we would show up with nine guys and look mediocre at best.

The roster continued to take some hits as the season went on, our Cuban defector, Carlos Benitez decided to give up baseball after he was passed up in the Major League draft, catcher Adam Frederick changed jobs and was relegated to weekend only duty, rookie pitcher Eric Hetrich decided to concentrate on his football career midway through the season, Nick Zerbe's internship eliminated him from the pitching rotation by mid-June, Leon Adams missed several weeks with kidney stones and coaching, work and school conflicts limited the duties of Rob Lozenski, Chad Denunzio, Dan Myers and Kyle Stover.

The obstacles kept popping up and we kept trying to overcome them.

By mid-June, just after we had captured our second Rawlings Berkshire Showdown title in the past three years, we were staring at a crucial week in the season where we wouldn't have a catcher.

Enter, my son-in-law, Stephen Croft who hadn't been on a Berkshire Red Sox active roster since the 2002 season. He was quickly given the nickname "Crash" by the younger guys on the team, who looked at him as our version of Crash Davis from the movie *Bull Durham*.

A four year lay-off, marriage, starting a photography business and two kids later, Stephen was behind the dish for us against the Smitty's Cardinals.

He proved to be a vital part in the clubs run down the stretch.

The rollercoaster ride continued all summer long, we would reach one milestone, such as achieving another 40 win season as early as June 30, recording my 500th career coaching victory on July 12 at Ephrata and setting a single season win mark with their 49th win of the season on July 17th and then we'd follow-up every big win with a crucial loss.

As we continued our late summer stretch, more bumps in the road had to be overcome.

By early July, another blow to our pitching staff would have to be overcome when Kevin Morganti went down with a season ending arm injury.

Parity in the Quad-County Optimist League that year kept us in the middle of the pack, but even with all of the set-backs that 2007 brought, we found ourselves within striking distance of the Regular Season title with four games to play in the final three days of our season.

A twi-night double-header sweep of Memory 21 on July 17, left us needing to win one of our next two games to capture the regular season title.

The following night, we lost to the Ephrata Blue Coats 3-2 with Nate Reed on the hill, but still just needed to knock off our brother squad, the Berkshire Blue Sox in our regular season finale the next night to capture the Regular Season title.

The Blue Sox on the other hand, would have to beat us and Lititz the following Monday in order for them to take the title and they did just that as they thumped us 5-1 and then went on to beat Lititz 2-1 to win the title.

In the five days that we were idle as the rest of the league finished up their regular season schedules, we slowly dropped from the number two seed to the number four seed in the play-offs as everyone who we needed to lose—won.

Losing the final two games of our season wasn't exactly the high note that we wanted heading into the post-season.

However, even with the late season collapse, we had a bit of resolve heading into the post-season knowing that if we got hot, we could beat anyone.

In the Quarterfinal opener, Nate Reed set the tone by tossing a no-hitter in a 3-1 series opening win against the Ephrata Blue Coats.

It took two days for us to beat the Blue Coats in game 2 and complete the sweep as rain suspended the contest and forced us to come back the next night as the we hung on to eliminate Ephrata 5-4.

In the Semifinals, we faced our rival, the PlayBall Black Sox and again set the tone early as we swept the Black Sox by scores of 7-3, 13-2 and 4-3 to secure an improbable fifth straight trip to the LCS.

In the League Championship Series, we faced a familiar, but yet unexpected foe in the Smitty's Cardinals.

Although, the Cardinals and us had squared off in the LCS in 2003, 2004 and 2005, we both had made it there as the number one and number two seeds entering the play-offs.

This year, we were the number four seed and the Cardinals needed a tie-breaker game against the Lititz Pirates just to secure the sixth and final seed of the post-season.

As I had mentioned before, we had taken the series in 2003 and the Cardinals came out on top in both 2004 and 2005.

We would again be looking to take control of the momentum in the series early and we did just that with a 12-3 win in game one at home at George Field.

The next night, we took a commanding two-games-none lead over the Cards with a 6-4 win.

Heading to Lancaster for game three and riding a seven game post-season winning streak, there was a lot of talk on the bus ride to the game about how the team would celebrate after the sweep.

Unfortunately, Smitty's was not about to go down without a fight and slapped us around that night on their way to a 7-4 win and forcing a game four in the best-of-five game series.

After the game, I had to remind our club that the year before, we were the ones down to that same Smitty's club 2-0 and came back to win the series. I had to make sure that they would be more focused the next night and complete the task at hand.

The following night, August 8, 2007, we did come out focused and determined and put the Cardinals away 7-3 to bring home our second straight league title and third in the past five years while notching a record breaking 59-23-1 record.

The thing that made that club special was that even with all of the injuries and all of the set-backs, someone different would step-up every night. We were very deep and had guys who understood their roles and were ready to go when we needed them. It was another true testament of what team work is all about.

As I said at the beginning of this chapter, to just pick a few of the great memories that I've had over twenty-plus years of coaching was an incredibly difficult task.

The game at Graterford was just a blast and a once in a lifetime experience, winning those back-to-back titles and that run from 2003 to 2007 was simply amazing and they had to be mentioned here.

However, I would have been miffed to not mention my 2011 Berkshire Sea Dogs team.

With the growth of our organization over the previous few years, my assistant coach since 2004, Brooke Kramer, one of my best friends, and I had determined that in the best interest of the organization, we should probably be on two different coaching staffs. This was one of the examples of being able to focus on the big picture and again being able to put the best interests of the organization in front of our own personal interests.

So for the 2011 season, Brooke continued coaching our 16-U Red Sox team while I moved down to coach our 14-U Sea Dogs team. As much as I really enjoyed coaching at the 16-U level, I knew that this was the decision that was in the best interest of the organization.

As it turned out, that 2011 fall season with the 14-U Sea Dogs was like a breath of fresh air for me and my coaching career. We didn't win a tournament championship and our final record was 25-18, but this was an exceptional group of young men and a great group of parents as well.

As any fourteen-year- old team will do, we had our share of highs and lows throughout the season. We played a little inconsistently at times, but we had great chemistry and this group of kids and their parents really bought into what we were looking to accomplish as a team and as an organization.

We only had twelve players on the roster and we battled injuries all season long, never having all twelve players healthy at the same time. It was one of those teams that at the end of the season, you sit and ask yourself, "…what if?"

We won 25 games and earned one tournament runner-up finish with being banged up all year, what if we would have been healthy? What if we wouldn't have had a freak October snowstorm? What if we would have had better weather?

When these kids were focused and running on all cylinders, they were something special. The best part of coaching at the 14-year- old level is that you have to stay on your toes and make sure that the players are focused. They can be so easily distracted at that age, but when you get that correct mixture, it is fun to watch.

Arguably, one of our best players, Aaron Gentry showed incredible character throughout the 2011 season. He was injured at the end of his summer season and started our fall season nursing the same injury. I can only wish that Aaron learned as much from me that season as I did from him. Aaron is a fierce competitor and has a lot of natural talent. It killed him to have to sit and watch while he was hurt, but he proved that even while hurt, he was a true leader and the ultimate teammate. He was always at our games, in uniform and did whatever he could to help the team even without being able to play. He always kept a positive attitude and helped his teammates in any way that he could.

He was chomping at the bit to get on the field and there were many times that I had to remind him that in the grand scheme of things, his health was still the most important issue for us to address. It makes me sick to know that many other coaches at that level would have been pushing to get him back onto the field even if he wasn't one-hundred percent in order to help pick-up that almighty win. I had to keep reigning Aaron in and make him understand that to miss one more game was a minor set-back as opposed to rushing back and missing another twenty-plus games. About mid-way through our season, I just had to tell him to stop apologizing to me that he couldn't play. It really wasn't that big of a deal to me as opposed to making sure that when he did get back onto the field that it was going to be for the long haul.

That again is the beauty of coaching this game, when you have a season like that and you think of all of the special things that might have happened with a break or two, it also gives you solace in knowing that that group of kids worked hard and listened to what you had to say as a coach. Even though you will not be in the dugout when they do win that title and when they are one-hundred percent healthy, both you and they will know what part of that success that you had played a part in.

So every time that I think of that 2011 14-U Sea Dogs team with Kyle Gantert, Aaron Gentry, Joe Rozzi, Anthony Juhasz, Zach Sermarini, Zavier Webb, Nick Behm, Jackie Diem, Kody Klopp, Cameron Weidner, Brandon Campbell and Tucker Douglas it will always bring a smile to my face.

The best part of that 2011 season was when I received the book, *Anatomy of Baseball* and a thank you card from one of my catchers, Zach Sermarini, the card read:

Hi Coach Dan,

Thank you so much for all of your advice and help this fall. I learned so much from you, and I will never forget this season. You have helped make me a better baseball player, and ultimately, have shaped me as a better young man.

Again, thank you so much for coaching me this season, and I look forward to seeing you at the winter workouts.

P.S. – I thought you would really enjoy this book.

~Zach

So after saying so many times throughout this book about how you have to realize that as a coach, you're planting seeds and sometimes it may be years or even decades before you actually see the fruits of your labor, I must admit that for those few times when you do see a little bit of instant gratification, it sure feels great.

Those are the memories of the game that will last a lifetime.

CHAPTER 14

Never Stop Learning

*I*f there is one thing that I have learned in a lifetime of coaching baseball it is that I still have so much more to learn about coaching baseball. Not just the "X's and O's," but even how to deal with players, teams, and parents. In coaching almost fifteen hundred games over twenty-two years. I've realized that every team, every player has a distinct personality and that there is no cookie-cutter approach to handling any of them.

I've attended coaches' clinics, I've read books. I've done everything that I could to continue to educate myself throughout my coaching career.

Most of all, I have surrounded myself with people who have been successful in the game of baseball. I've been fortunate enough to be an associate scout for the Philadelphia Phillies since 2001 and that has afforded me the opportunity to meet and talk with some very successful individuals within the Phillies organization. It has also given me a pretty keen understanding into the player development department of a Major League baseball club, a system that we have tried to mirror within the Berkshire organization as closely as a youth amateur baseball organization can mirror a professional club.

One thing that I have learned throughout my life is that if you truly wish to be successful in a certain field, you should find someone who is already successful in that field and attempt to emulate what they have done to be successful.

Even when I was still selling building materials for Wickes Lumber, I became very close friends with our top salesman in the company, Dave Pard. I was selling about $4.3 million a year in building materials and Dave was selling about $14 million a year, I wanted to find out what he was doing to be successful and carry that over into my market. It only made sense to me and it's a method that I believe can be applied to every aspect of life. Regardless of the field of endeavor that you're looking to work in, find someone who is successful in that field and use that person as a mentor.

It's great to become a mentor to your players, but everyone needs to have a mentor as well. My mother was my mentor in so many aspects of my life, but I have many other mentors as well. There is no rule that says that you can only have one mentor in life. We all have so many people who can influence our lives; we need to take all of the positive things that our mentors teach us throughout our lives and mold them and shape them into our own styles and methods. It is truly what makes us individuals. We are all made up of so many different components and philosophies and we use the ones that have influenced us the most to create our own individuality.

The minute that we stop being influenced by others and stop learning is the minute that we stop living. It is a constant process and a constant evolution. It changes every minute. We always have to be receptive to new ideas and methods in the game and use bits and pieces of them to incorporate into our own style.

You can never become closed-minded and start to believe that you know everything that there is to know about the game. By the same token, you do have to create your own methods, styles and philosophies about the game through the elements that you've learned through others. The coach that is always jumping on the latest bandwagon and philosophy of the game ultimately brings very little to the table as well. You have to have some sort of substance and common thread to what you teach and what you believe in. Your own personal convictions must ultimately be stronger than every DVD that you watch or book that you read. You must keep some type of continuity in your teaching or your players will quickly pick up on the fact that you're simply blowing smoke.

The fundamentals of the game have not changed in over a hundred years so there is no reason to attempt to reinvent the game. Keep it simple, keep it basic, and always make sure that the reason that you're doing this is for the betterment of the players that you're coaching. Career records, wins and losses, championships, and accolades will take care of themselves if you're truly coaching for the right reasons.

Your best interests and concerns must always take a backseat to the best interests and concerns of the teams and your players.

Always remember that you truly are a role model and a great influence on your players' lives, whether that influence is positive or negative, it is still a great influence.

CHAPTER 15

Pay Back Time

*T*here is no greater gift in the world than to give of yourself to help someone else. As I had mentioned before, my mom believed that helping others was her own form of "payback time." I guess because of her, I may have been doomed from the start to be so concerned about helping others and truly feeling blessed to be able to do so.

Both of my parents were extremely giving individuals. My father was an over-the-road truck driver, so he never had much time to give. What he lacked in being able to donate in time, he donated in money instead. My mother, on the other hand, had very little money to spare for the majority of her life, I'm not convinced that she had a lot of time either, but somehow she managed to fit it all in. As I mentioned in the beginning of the book, after my mother and father separated, my mother and I moved to Florida. This was not an easy time for us. She was a single mother, in the late 1970s and early 1980s during the midst of the energy crisis, trying to make the best for her and her youngest son. To this day, I don't know how she pulled it off. It was a juggling act of epic proportions to say the least. The funniest thing of all is that at the time,

I had no clue what was even going on. I never felt that we were needy at all. We never missed a meal, I always made it to every Little League game and practice, and she was always there to root me on or work in the concession stand. This was all on top of working at least three jobs most of the time. I can remember for sure at one time, she was selling life insurance as a full-time job, working as a waitress in the evening at two different restaurants, and doing construction cleaning on the weekends. With all that, she still found time for me and for anyone else who needed a hand.

If that influence from my mother and father in its own right hadn't been enough for me to have it totally ingrained in my soul to help others, my grandfather certainly topped it off. When I went to visit my father in Pennsylvania for the summers after my mom and dad had gotten divorced, I would spend the weekdays at my grandparents' house because my dad was driving a truck. My dad's father, Elwood Clouser, was another incredible influence on me when it came to understanding the importance of helping others. My grandfather volunteered at our church, literally all the time. He would wake me up at 5:00 a.m. on a Friday morning to take me along to help set up for a church yard sale. I guess I was cheap labor at the time. At thirteen and fourteen years old I had a bunch of energy and I guess my grandfather just didn't want to see it go to waste. I went along many times kicking and screaming, but to spend the day with my grandfather was well worth it. Regardless of how much energy I had in those days, I still had to bring my A game to keep up with my grandfather; he was one of the hardest working individuals that I've ever met.

So it was with that upbringing that volunteering became pretty much second nature for me as I grew up.

Unfortunately, volunteerism in today's world is almost a lost art. Today, most people are more concerned about what's in it for them as opposed to just going and helping someone without expecting anything in return. I see it repeatedly within our own organization. Because of the costs that are involved in participating in our program, we conduct several fundraisers throughout the year where our parents are literally fundraising for themselves to help offset their child's travel costs. Because Berkshire Baseball is a nonprofit 501(c)3 corporation, it allows our parents the liberty to raise funds that will help them offset their registration costs that consist mostly of their travel expenses. Most of the fundraising is optional; if they choose not to fundraise, then they end up paying for the trip costs and registration costs out of their pockets. Generally, we get a good response from the parents to help raise funds, especially considering the fact that they are essentially raising the funds for themselves.

We also conduct fundraisers and run concession stands during our tournaments to help offset our administrative costs and more importantly benefit our scholarship fund and our World Equipment Outreach Project. What amazes me is that we probably get fewer than ten percent of our parents and players to participate when the fundraiser does not directly benefit them. Coming from a background where I saw my mom and grandfather always give their time and my dad, who because of his job driving truck, never had much time, always gave monetarily, this is very hard for me to swallow.

When I hear parents say things like, "Why should we help in the concession stand?" it can make my blood boil. It shows me that they are very selfish and very shortsighted individuals. Again for someone like myself; who was taught from a very young age that giving of one's self was a way of life, it can be very difficult for me to understand. As I had mentioned previously, one year, I had hung photos of all of our players on the wall of our concession stand at the Robesonia Playground and I wrote the caption, "THIS IS WHY..." above the photos of our players. I was always the first one at the field and the last one to leave. I am human and there would always be those days when I may have been a little tired in the morning, even more tired at the end the day, or just generally grumpy; those pictures with that caption always served as a reminder to me about why I did what I did. It's actually amazing how well it worked, tired and grumpy, I'd look at that caption and those faces on the wall and I would get a second wind. Although coaching and volunteering is quite a thankless job for the most part, it's the seeds that you plant that serve as your motivation. This is certainly not an instant gratification journey, and that is what you have to remember to keep going. They may not appreciate what you do today, they may not appreciate what you do tomorrow, but believe me, they will appreciate it someday.

Coaching baseball is just a way for me to give of myself. It is one small way for me to pay back those who helped me out in the game of baseball and more importantly the game of life. From my first two Little League coaches in the Oley Valley Youth League, Coach Heist and Coach Distasio, to my coaches Dan Gordon, Dennis Blair, and Denny Werner at Schuylkill Valley Junior High School and High School, respectfully, and all of the others in between, they all taught me something. They taught me to play the game, but more importantly, they taught me how to be a good person both on and off the field. However, as I have already said so many times in this book, baseball has been the tool; teaching life is what the greater achievement is.

One thing that I will never forget occurred back in 2006. We had just started our new 12-U program the previous year and the gentlemen who had coached the team for the first season, coached for only that first year and then had to step down. So for the 2006 season, Jimmy Everhart, who had played in the organization with us since 2000 and served as an assistant on the 12-U staff the year before, was now at the helm. Jimmy was young, just graduated college the year before, but I knew he would be a great coach. I had had the privilege of coaching Jimmy on our collegiate-aged team during the summers while he was still playing at St. Michaels College in Vermont. He was just one of those types of kids, who just played the game. He did whatever he was asked to do and did it well. He never complained about anything. He was a catcher by trade and did some pitching for us as well. He was one of the smartest players that I had ever coached. As a catcher, he was almost part of my coaching staff already during the summer. He was my eyes and ears to the pitching staff and knew exactly how to call a game.

When we host a tournament, we literally use fields that are spread across our entire county. We try to keep fields together that have the same age groups playing, but throughout the entire tournament, we literally have fields all over. This particular season, the 12-U teams would play at a field that was located about five minutes from my house. My 16-U team played most of their weekends at a field that was located about five minutes from Jimmy's house. The issue is that Jimmy and I lived about forty-five minutes from each other so this wonderful scheduling would have each of us driving about forty-five minutes to get to the field that we were playing at. The only good thing about that setup that turned out to be beneficial was that Jimmy and I would generally meet at a Sunoco station that was located about halfway between our two fields most Saturday mornings so that I could give him baseballs, trophies, T-shirts and other supplies for the weekend. This meeting would generally take place at about 6:00 a.m. so that we could both get to our fields in plenty of time to get them prepped and ready for the day.

One particular day, I was running a little behind schedule, so I called Jimmy around 5:30 that morning to let him now that I might be a few minutes late. As we were talking, I jokingly said to him, "So I guess you're regretting the day that you signed up for this job, huh?" Considering it was 5:30 on a Saturday morning, I knew that most kids Jimmy's age had probably just rolled into bed a few hours ago.

Jimmy's response simply floored me when he said, "Well, Dan, I really don't mind it all. I mean, I already know that you're up early to go get a baseball field ready for somebody to play on, Brooke's already up to go get a baseball field ready for somebody to play on, and during my entire life, my Dad was up early every weekend to go get a baseball field ready for someone else to play on. I guess it just wouldn't be right if I wasn't up this early on a Saturday or Sunday morning to go get a field ready for someone else to play on."

Those words came from a twenty-three-year-old kid. I was amazed and extremely proud all at the same time. This kid truly understood what coaching was all about and what giving of one's self is all about. His parents instilled an incredibly solid work ethic and set of values in him. Unfortunately, that was Jimmy's last year coaching in our organization because he relocated to the Boston area shortly after our season ended. We stay in touch to this day, get together when he comes home to see his family, and anytime that I get up to a Red Sox game, I try to at least have dinner with him and his girlfriend. He is a solid young man and our organization lost someone very good when he relocated. On the other hand, the Boston area benefitted tremendously, as Jimmy coaches several different junior high sports at the school where he teaches. Jimmy Everhart completely understood what payback time really meant.

In January of 2006, almost a year to the date that my mother had passed away, my wife and I went on a cruise with my brother and his wife, Kathy, and two of our other friends, Steve and Leslie McKibbon. Our one port of call on the cruise was Roatan, Honduras. Roatan is a small island about forty miles north of the mainland of Honduras. In 2006 at least, it was still very underdeveloped and not nearly as much of a tourist trap as most of the other ports on the cruise. Steve and Leslie were the two "cruising veterans" of our group, but this was the first cruise for my wife and I as well as for Don and Kathy, so we pretty much did whatever Steve and Leslie suggested when we arrived at a port. Steve pretty much went scuba diving everywhere we stopped and Roatan was no different. As I had said, Roatan wasn't nearly as built up as the other ports that we had stopped at, so tourist attractions were limited. Somewhere prior to the cruise Leslie had heard of an orphanage down there, called Child Sponsorship International through some of her other friends. The orphanage had an arrangement with many cruise lines, and several "cruisers" would often bring supplies to them such as toiletries and clothing. After hearing about this, Leslie had gathered up a few suitcases of stuff that she brought on the cruise to take to the orphanage that day. Leslie asked all of us if we'd be interested in going with her to the orphanage and we all agreed.

It was kind of a rainy day on the island that day and the five of us squeezed into a small van that the director of the orphanage, Brad Warren, had arranged to pick us up at the port. As we arrived at the orphanage, it was raining hard, so we all scurried into the house and Brad started to introduce us to the children. As the rain slowed down and eventually stopped, Brad started to give us a tour of the facility. As we were finishing the tour and were heading back into the main house, my brother and I noticed a wide open flat grassy area of land in the front of the orphanage. My brother, who is as much of a soccer fanatic as I am a baseball fanatic, immediately asked Brad if the open area was going to be a soccer field. Considering that we were in Central America, even I would have thought soccer first. Brad's response surprised all of us, when he told us that they were going to be building a baseball field there, not a soccer field. Obviously, my interest in this project was now piqued.

As we continued to talk about the baseball field, I mentioned to Brad my involvement in Berkshire Baseball and that I felt that we might be able to help them out in some small way by gathering some equipment and getting it to them. This was the official birth of our organizations World Equipment Outreach Program. Brad was excited at the thought, considering he didn't really have any equipment to speak of at this juncture and that places that we take for granted in the United States like sporting goods chain stores were nonexistent in Honduras. As we spoke and interacted with the kids at the orphanage that day, my passion for this new project grew even stronger. To see how grateful these kids were to just have someone to play checkers with them was incredibly touching to all of us. Being thankful and grateful for what we have in the United States was just a bonus of the visit in general.

At our first board meeting once we arrived back in the States, I presented the idea to our board of directors. Once we passed the motion to start the project, we starting scheduling collection dates and sites across the county and we quickly generated a slew of nice equipment to be sent.

The one thing that I was adamant about when presenting the idea to our board was that we also wanted to find an organization locally to be a beneficiary to the program as well. With that in mind, we partnered with the Olivet Boys & Girls Club of Reading and Berks County, which had just recently started their RBI program. It bothers me that our government sends billions of dollars to other countries as foreign aid but neglects the millions of homeless, jobless, and starving people right here in our own backyard. That doesn't make much sense to me at all. I have no issues with the richest country in the world helping those countries that are less fortunate than ours, but we can't lose sight of home either. That was a primary focus of this project, to be able to make an impact both locally and internationally and we have certainly accomplished that over the years.

Since the initial inception of the program in 2006, we have collected and distributed over four hundred boxes of used baseball and softball equipment both locally and throughout the world. We have since also partnered with the *National Alliance of Youth Sports* and their *Global Gear Drive Program* so that now the equipment that we collect can be distributed on a much broader scope across the world as opposed to just one orphanage in Roatan, Honduras.

Again, for some people, this entire concept can be very difficult to understand as to why we would spend so much time, money, and energy on such a project. However, once you get the chance to hand a new or used baseball glove to a child who never in a million years would have had the means to get one otherwise, and you see the look of gratitude in those young eyes, you would understand completely.

In 2011, we had an extremely rainy year. At the end of the season, we probably had between three and four thousand dollars of leftover concession food that we had no idea what to do with.

One of our parents suggested at a board meeting to donate the items to the food bank. As some time had passed and we still had not made a final decision on what to do with the food, an opportunity arose that allowed us to take part in an event that was called "Cups of Compassion" here in Reading, Pennsylvania. The premise of the idea was for a few people to get together and make some soup to give away on the street to those in need in our local community.

When we heard about the project, we suggested that we add some hamburgers, hot dogs, snacks, and drinks to the menu and the organizers jumped at the opportunity to have us participate.

This was again, a chance for us to make an impact as an organization to the "end user," a much more emotional experience for those who participated as opposed to just taking the leftover food to a warehouse and dropping it off.

Again, when you see the look in someone's eyes who you have genuinely helped, words simply cannot explain the emotions that come from giving back.

As I've done so many times already in this book, I'll share with you the article that I wrote shortly after the event that we published in our e-newsletter on December 22, 2011...

BERKSHIRE BASEBALL PITCHES IN TO HELP THOSE IN NEED AT "CUPS OF COMPASSION" EVENT

One of the proudest moments in the rich 22-year history of Berkshire Baseball took place on Tuesday, December 20, 2011, and we were miles away from the nearest baseball field.

Berkshire Baseball has been a member of the Greater Reading Convention & Visitors Bureau since 2001 and I've personally served on the GRCVB board since 2009.

Tuesday, a few members of Berkshire Baseball, along with the help of many other organizations, businesses and volunteers in the Reading and Berks County community came together to help those in need by serving free food at the corner of 5th and Penn streets in Reading.

The idea was the brainchild of Annette Church of The Gallery Above the Square and Laura Cooper of Liberty Law Group.

Our organization was fortunate to become involved when Crystal Seitz, President of the GRCVB sent out an e-mail to her board looking for some support with the event.

Originally started as an event that would offer a free cup of soup and bread, we had another idea to help.

With our last tournament of the season being cancelled by a freak October blizzard, our organization was left with the question of what in the world were we going to do with all of the leftover food and drinks that we had from the concession stands at each field?

At our November board meeting, when the topic came up for discussion, Hope Distasio, mother of Nick Distasio, a player on our 16-U Berkshire Blue Sox team suggested that we donate the left-over food to the Greater Reading and Berks Food Bank. Thinking that was a great idea, but also having to finalize our banquet, coaches clinic and details on our upcoming winter clinics, the food remained in the freezers of board members and parents throughout Berks County.

I guess sometimes everything happens for a reason, so when I received Crystal's e-mail about the Cups of Compassion event, the wheels in my head immediately started to turn. The strangest thing is that I was actually considering conducting a similar event ourselves with our extra food, after I had read the Secret Santa article in the paper a few weeks back. Again, I guess things really do happen for a reason.

So I forwarded Crystal's e-mail to our board asking for their thoughts on donating our leftover concession items and having some members come out that morning and help grill. It was a no-brainer and everything just started to fall into place from there.

Once our board approved the idea, I ran it by Crystal and Annette because the initial request was for soups and we were a little outside of the soup theme with burgers, dogs, chips, snacks, and drinks. The idea was embraced and we were off to the races a little over a week prior to the event to put everything into place.

We started coordinating how to get all of the food from the freezers that it was currently in, to the event and gathered up a few volunteers to help with the day of the event. The only items that we did not have for the event were the rolls, which Stroemann Bakeries graciously donated to the cause.

So Tuesday morning at 7:30 AM, Boo Schaeffer and Mike Billera-Smith met at the Berks County Youth Recreational Facility and loaded our big grill onto Boo's truck and headed into the city. I stopped at my daughter and son-in-law's house to get food from their freezer and then again at FirstEnergy Stadium to meet Dan Douglas and get the remaining food that the Reading Phillies had been gracious enough to allow us to store in one of their big freezers.

Then I was off to the city, where Bill Hartranft and Hope and Natalia Distasio met us to get our portion of the event set up.

As soon as I arrived, I could feel something special in the air. There was a buzz and a feeling that we were all helping and pulling together to do our small part to help get this great city back to the prosperous place that it once was.

Members of the Downtown Improvement District were scurrying around since 6:30 in the morning setting up tables and chairs and prepping for the event.

No one was standing around, we were all greeting each other with smiles and hugs and grabbing coolers and crock pots to get set up and get ready to go.

From the time that we threw our first burgers and dogs on the grill around 8:30 AM, the people started to line up and the line went on for hours. The original timeframe for the event was 9:00 AM to 11:00 AM, but we determined that we'd serve until the food ran out, which was somewhere around 12:30 PM.

We served nonstop for four hours, I only had about a five minute break when I could peak around the corner and see the action at the other serving stations and was simply amazed by how this group pulled together for the common good of our community.

The gratitude of those who benefited from this event was simply overwhelming. They were all smiling and happy and truly grateful for our efforts. Many telling us how this was their first hot meal in a week or more. They filled up on soup and hamburgers and hot dogs today and many stocked up on our Slim Jim's or a bag of chips, saying that that would be tomorrow's meal.

Words cannot express the feeling that you get when helping in a situation like that. You feel awesome that you're able to make someone's day, but by the same token, you're incredibly frustrated by knowing that you're just scratching the surface of a much larger problem. The nice part about working the grill for four hours was that no one could tell if my eyes were watering because of battling the smoke from the grill or from battling my emotions.

The power of a few e-mails gripped a community if only for a few hours, but it will last a lifetime for many. To think about the number of people that we touched in those few hours was impressive. The thought of what we'll be able to do in the future is really overwhelming.

The GRCVB only reached out to its board members, our own organization only reached out to our board members and the parent whose idea snowballed. Everything came to together so quickly, that my initial thought was to reach out to our general membership for support and that never happened. I truly apologize to all those parents who have told me since Tuesday that they wish that they would've known about the event because they would have loved to help and I assure you that you will know about it well in advance for 2012.

I am sure that this event will become a benchmark of the resilience and compassion that exists in Reading, Pennsylvania and I am so grateful to Annette, Laura and Crystal for allowing our organization to be a small part of such a powerful event and look forward to helping it get even better in the future.

So I guess that is it, which is what it is all about. That is the "payback time" that I am referring to. Whether you want to call it paying it forward or paying it back, it makes no difference either way. The important thing to understand is that everyone in this world has been helped by someone along the way. No one here can simply go at it alone. We may try from time to time, but we all depend on someone else to help us somewhere along the way. The sooner we all understand that, the world will be a much better place.

CHAPTER 16

Mr. Potter, I Think I Have Your Answer

As I've mentioned many times before, Jeff Potter has been an individual who has been very instrumental in my motivation to get this book completed. To say this has been a work in progress is a drastic understatement and honestly, if it were not for Jeff Potter and him making me understand the "fear of failure" and committing to complete this project, it may very well still be on my computer's hard drive and never published.

Jeff's book is titled *Whatever Happened to Baseball?* and I think that I may have discovered the answer. However, the title of his book could just as easily been *Whatever Happened to Society?* As mentioned so many times before in this book, baseball is a reflection on life; therefore, baseball is also a reflection on society. So the real question is whatever happened to society? How could we have traveled so far for so long, and yet in many ways we have been traveling in reverse without even knowing it.

Most of things that are problems in baseball today are still our biggest problems in society.

So many of the things that I have mentioned in this book that make the game of baseball so great, are the exact same things that are missing from so many youth organizations today.

We've become so selfish these days, on and off the field. Our decision-making process is a reflection of a "what is best for me" attitude, regardless of how that decision affects my teammates. The sacrifice bunt has become one of the most unpopular plays in the game of baseball, because the concept of one person making a genuine sacrifice for the good of his team or to help a teammate advance to the next base is totally unheard of anymore in our society, let alone on the baseball field. How can we possibly get a young person to grasp the concept of sacrificing on a baseball field when everything they see in everyday life is telling them to do what is best for themselves, regardless of how it may affect others?

Everywhere you look in society today, kids see decisions being made with a "me first" philosophy. The bankers and mortgage brokers that created the housing bubble in the 1990s and 2000s knew that it would come crumbling down around them. But their decision-making process was about how much money they could make, not whether or not the young couple that could barely afford the mortgage payment that they had just signed on for could afford it in three years when their adjustable rate payment increases by another $200 a month. It didn't matter, there was money to be made and it was being made by flying on the coattails of "living the American Dream."

This American dream was a by-product of the instant gratification and entitlement that our society has become accustomed to. The days of people working hard and saving money for several years so that they could afford to purchase a house with a 20 percent down payment had vanished. It was now time for the twenty-something-year-old kid, fresh out of college with $100,000 in student loans to go out and purchase a $200,000 house with $3,000 in down payment money. The same thought process has transitioned onto the baseball field as well. The thought of the freshman in high school or college getting cut from the team and then spending the entire off-season working his ass off to get better so that he can make the team as a sophomore are gone. The trend now is to transfer immediately to a school where you can play. Working hard to get better is a dinosaur philosophy in this day and age.

Travel baseball, or "Daddy Baseball," as I like to refer to it, in most cases is the same way. There are literally hundreds of thousands of teams out there now and thousands of new ones pop up every year, started by some dad whose son wasn't good enough to start on the team he played for last season. Dad starts his own team so that "little Johnny" can be the starting short-stop and bat clean-up in the lineup every day. To even suggest to a player's father that his son should spend the off-season working hard so that he can compete for a starting position the following year will in many cases get you lynched in this day and age.

Another issue in today's game and society is that everyone wants to be the star of the team. In reality, that simply is not how life works. There is no one left who is content with being the role-player on a roster and when you get right down to it, in most cases, the role-player is oftentimes the most important guy on the roster. He knows how important he is and his teammates certainly know his importance to the team's success, but everyone wants to see their name in the headlines nowadays. Again, everyone wants to be Michael Jordan; no one wants to be Scottie Pippen. People are quick to forget that *teams* win championships, not individual players. Most kids nowadays would prefer to be the star of a lousy team as opposed to the role-player on a championship team—a sad reality of the times in which we now live.

The uneducated fan thinks that that Carlton Fisk was the hero for the Boston Red Sox in Game 6 of the 1975 World Series, the members of the Red Sox and the fan with any type of baseball sense realizes that without Bernie Carbo, Fisk would never have gotten his chance to hit the game winner.

The same can be said for Game 4 of the ALCS in 2004. The everyday fan thinks that David Ortiz was the hero; the organization knows that without Dave Roberts, it's just another miserable heartbreaking loss for an organization that had been snake-bitten for eighty-six years and would have been longer without Dave Roberts.

When I was a junior in high school, I was one of four juniors that made the varsity baseball team. We had a very talented senior class and those twelve seniors were most definitely going to see the majority of the playing time. Within a week after the team selections were made, the other three juniors went to our coach and asked if they could be sent down to the JV team for the year because they'd get more playing time on the JV team. Our coach granted their request and then approached me to see if I wanted to do the same. I declined because I knew that that group of seniors had a chance to do something very special that year. I also knew that I wouldn't see the field very often either, but that wasn't what was important to me. What was important was to possibly be part of a championship team, regardless of what my role was, I just wanted to help out and learn from the other players on that roster.

I got four at-bats that season; we won the Division Championship and finished second in the County, while advancing to the quarterfinals of the district play-offs. I never had any regrets about that decision. I would have probably started the entire season on the JV team, just as I had as a sophomore, but the opportunity to be a part of that 1986 team at Schuylkill Valley High School, I wouldn't trade for the world. It was a very special experience.

Another missing component in today's society and our great game of baseball is that great quality called commitment that I spent an entire chapter on earlier in the book.

It also roots back to the "me first" attitude. The decision-making process that affects only your own best interests. The very thought of actually making a commitment to an organization in this day and age is virtually unheard of.

In today's world, the average American will hold 11.4 jobs during a working lifetime, compared to the 1970s when the average American would hold five jobs during a lifetime. Again, this issue with our society has carried over to the baseball field. Don't get me wrong, I'm not trying to say that every person that changes jobs has an issue with commitment, but speaking about the vast majority, that is a direct reflection of a generation's lack of commitment to an organization or always thinking that the grass is greener on the other side of the fence.

Our national divorce rate is another example of our lack of commitment in this generation. People do not know how to work out their issues, a marriage is always a work in progress, yet for so many people, it's so much easier to leave than it is to stick around and work out your issues. Marriage is a give and take, I know that if my wife was looking for someone better than me, she could certainly find him, but she made a choice, as did I, that we'd spend our lives together. It hasn't always been rosy, but we both shared the same opinion that it was worth the work that we needed to put into it to make it last. My wife is ten years older than I am, so many people thought that our relationship would not last, but it has. It has lasted for twenty-three years now and it is stronger now than it ever has been because we've made a commitment to each other to do whatever it takes to make it work.

This is something that many people struggle with when it comes to their child's youth baseball experience. The only commitment that they have is to themselves, and their decision-making process revolves only around their own best interests.

We had a prime example of this one year when we had a family who chose to have their son go play for another team for an extended weekend while leaving our team shorthanded for five to six games over the summer. No matter how I tried to explain it to the mother, she simply did not care that she was teaching her son that it was OK to leave the team that he had played with all summer to go play for another team for the weekend. The decision was solely based on what they felt was best for their son and there was absolutely no regard to leaving the team shorthanded that he had played almost forty games with.

It amazes me how when you actually call people out in a situation like that, instead of taking responsibility for their actions, they prefer to try to justify their actions by pointing out other team members' shortcomings and lack of commitment as well. This was something that I simply cannot grasp. It's kind of like trying to plea with a judge in a murder trial that because others have committed murder and have gotten away with it, why can't you? I guess the two wrongs don't make it right theory is a thing of the past as well.

At some point, you have to just step back and realize that no matter what you say, some people will attempt to find their own justification in their decision. When you know that decision is being made solely out of selfish intentions, they simply won't get it when you start talking about commitment and being loyal to their teammates and an organization. You just have to accept the fact that building a youth baseball organization on principles such as good sportsmanship, honesty, loyalty, dignity, humility, class, and respect for authority is a very unpopular stance in today's world. You have to realize that in some cases it's just better to part ways. At that point, you can only hope that someday while looking in that mirror, a light bulb may go off and they'll figure it out.

The entire theory of the "hired gun" or "baseball mercenary" at the youth level is something that paints such a terrible picture to the young people of today. We wonder why there is no commitment, yet we teach no commitment by telling our young people that it is OK for them to weigh their options and figure out what is best for them by going from team to team on any given weekend. By never giving them the opportunity to understand what it means to be part of a team, they view their teammates as simply a necessary evil, eight additional young men that are required in order for them to fulfill their fix of a weekend tournament championship. We see it every weekend when we run a tournament, three "studs" who have been "on call" being delivered just in time for the start of a championship game, it's disgusting, yet so common in today's world. What are we really teaching our children?

So these are some of the things to help answer Jeff's question about whatever happened to baseball and more importantly, whatever happened to society?

The bigger question is what do we do to change the trend? In this time that we live in, how can we possibly change the "me first" philosophy that exists in sports and society today?

The answer is actually very simple, yet very difficult to implement. Please do not misunderstand when I point out all of the shortcomings of our youth sports society today, I'm painting with a very broad stroke; some very good organizations still exist in the world today, but they are most definitely in the minority. Way too many organizations out there are driven by money and giving players and parents false hopes of Division I scholarships and draft status as opposed to simply making kids understand that they need to work hard and enjoy the game for as long as they can. If they are extremely fortunate, they can have an opportunity to play this game in college or perhaps professionally.

So back to my simple answer: just keep doing things the right way and for the right reasons, regardless of how unpopular they may be.

I guess this answer is best described in an article that I wrote for the Berkshire Baseball program book in 2011, so rather than reinventing the wheel, I'll simply reprint that article here as well…

OLD-SCHOOL VALUES IN A
NEW-SCHOOL WORLD

When Berkshire Baseball was formed 22 years ago, we never had some grand vision that we would someday be sponsoring over 20 teams and hosting tournaments for teams all up and down the East Coast while making an economic impact of over a million dollars a year for the local Reading and Berks County area. We pretty much just wanted to play baseball. However, even in the beginning, as very young men, we knew that there was a certain "code of ethics" that the game needed to be played by. A respect for the game, a respect for your opponent and respect for the officials that needed to be adhered to. Play hard between the lines and leave it on the field, no matter what. Be committed and do what was best for the team first.

We understood and took it very seriously that there was a certain level of responsibility that went with wearing a Berkshire uniform and knew from the very beginning that we didn't want to be just another baseball organization. We wanted to set the bar very high from the beginning and make the "Berkshire Way" a way of good sportsmanship, honesty, loyalty, dignity, humility, class and respect for authority.

We wanted to be involved in the community and give back in any small way that we could and we did. Our influence and arm in the community has reached further than any of us could have ever imagined.

In 22 years, a lot has changed in baseball and society. In this day and age of "Daddy Ball" and "me first" it becomes extremely difficult at times to continue to instill some of those old-school values in today's new age ballplayer.

We live in a world where young people are coddled and parents have a hard time letting them go off to learn from their own mistakes. I still see parents carry their son's baseball bags for them as they go into their junior and senior year of high school. Kids are taught to make decisions that only affect themselves, regardless of how that decision may negatively affect their team.

Although building a large organization that is based on old-school values can sometimes seem like a monumental task in today's world, we as an organization still feel strongly that it is worth the extra work. If it was easy, everyone would do it.

We have grown tremendously over the past few years, every year we add some players and parents that simply do not "get it." At the end of each year, we have to go through the weeding out process to make sure that the core players for the following year are the right fit for the organization. We live by the Lou Holtz philosophy that we are not necessarily looking for the best players, but we're looking for the right players. Every year, no matter how much literature we provide or times that we tell people, we still always seem to get a few people who come in thinking that their 12- or 13-year-old son is "elite" or some sort of "super star" and think that they can go about their conduct on and off the baseball field with a different set of rules than that of their teammates. They learn fast that we actually hold our best players to a higher standard and expect them to lead by example.

Over the years, we have also had some coaches who have come into the organization thinking that their win/loss record supersedes their conduct on and off the field as well. Again their tenures are generally short-lived and we look to get coaches who are the right fit for the organization in place.

This is a constant work in progress. We, as an organization can never be content with ourselves. We need to constantly be monitoring the product that we put out and understand that not one individual is greater than the organization as a whole.

The success of our organization is not always measured in wins and losses, but more importantly by the impact that we as coaches, administrators and an organization as a whole have on the lives of the young men that go through our system. Most times those results cannot be measured until years after a young man's playing days with us are over. When he comes back to coach in the organization as so many have or when he just comes back to visit and you see what a successful member of society he has become. A good parent, a good husband, a successful businessman, those are the measure's of a youth sports organizations success.

So many times in youth sports today our morals are compromised. Sportsmanship takes a backseat, teamwork takes a backseat and discipline most certainly takes a back seat more often than not. The super star ballplayer is many times given a separate set of rules than his teammates and therefore learns nothing regarding leadership and responsibility.

We tell people all the time that Berkshire Baseball is not for everyone and we are very fortunate that we do have a very solid base of families and players who do still believe in old-school morals and that giving back is an important part of our existence here on earth.

In 22 years we have seen many organizations come and go. I imagine that we will see many more come and go over the next 22 years. Berkshire Baseball has stood the test of time and will continue to stand the test of time because the principles and values by which this organization was founded are real and are of substance. These old-school values have stood the test of time no matter how unpopular they sometimes are in this day and age and therefore so will Berkshire Baseball.

So there is your answer, just do the right thing for the right reasons. As a perfectionist, it is extremely frustrating for me to know that many people will not "buy into" this philosophy and that every year we have to go through our organization and "weed out" those who are not the right fit for the organization. I oftentimes get caught up in the number of families that we lose and ask myself and our board what we could have done differently to keep them. But the cold hard truth is that we will not keep them all, certainly not by promoting the philosophy and beliefs that we promote as an organization. So I have to go back and accept the fact that these are unpopular beliefs, but they are the correct beliefs and they are the beliefs that build an organization that can weather any storm and truly stand the test of time.

Those who are the right fit will make us prouder than we could have ever imagined.

CHAPTER 17

2010

$\mathcal{I}$t's always funny to me how things always end up working out for the best. As I had mentioned earlier in the book, I began this project in 2003, and after meeting Jeff Potter in 2009, I set a hard deadline for myself to have it completed by January 2010. That didn't happen and I was very disappointed. Now, with hindsight being twenty-twenty, I am very thankful that I missed the initial "deadline" that I had set for myself. If this book had been published in January of 2010, this chapter would have been left out and that would have been a shame, because there was a lot for me to learn in 2010 and those lessons need to be passed on.

Before I get to the early part of 2010, let me fast-forward to the end of 2010 and what I consider a defining moment in my life and my coaching career.

On Christmas Eve, I received a voice mail from one of my former players, Kyle Stover. When I called Kyle back, he informed me that his grandfather, Bill, had passed away. This was very sad news for me. I had coached Kyle off and on from when he was fifteen years old until he was about twenty-three years old. Kyle even helped coach our 18-U showcase team after he graduated college and I'm convinced that if he hadn't moved to Pittsburgh, he would still be heavily involved in the organization today. Kyle was one of those players that you love to coach. He was talented, but even more, he had that passion, and he worked hard on and off the field. He'd run through a wall for you. He wasn't the biggest guy or the strongest guy on the team, but he made up for his size in grit and heart. One of Kyle's best traits was his positive energy. He loved being at the baseball field, he loved being involved in the game. If we had one game, he wanted to play two, if we had two games, he would want to play three.

When he first started playing for me, he was fifteen and played for me at Conrad Weiser. When he came back to play for me on our college age team, he was part of a championship team; he was a freshman in college and was a role-player during that first season. He filled in where we needed him to and he played a huge part in helping us win that championship. He matured into an everyday player and a leader on a team that won three championships over the course of five years. He didn't come in as a freshman expecting to start every game; he came in and understood his role, learned from the veterans that we had in 2003, and took over their roles as they left and helped us bring home titles in 2006 and 2007 as well. That team played in the League Championship Series for five straight years from 2003 through 2007; it was a special time and a special group of guys.

However, to really understand Kyle's passion and positive attitude, you have to look back even further. His parents, Rick and Cozy, and his grandparents, Bill and Marianne, were some of the most genuine and positive people that I have ever met in my life. They were all always laughing and always smiling. Especially Bill. I can honestly say that I have never seen this man without a smile on his face, and not just any smile, I mean a smile that could light up a room. A genuine and sincere smile all of the time, not fake or staged, the real thing. Regardless of the situation, Bill was smiling. This always impressed me.

The other great thing about Kyle's family was that they were always there. I can probably count on one hand the number of games that someone from Kyle's family wasn't at during the time that Kyle played for me. As with any team, there were some games and stretches during those five years, as good as we were, that we didn't play great baseball.

We went through some slumps. I'll never forget that after every loss, I would be somewhat grumpy and as I would walk out of the dugout one of the first people that I would see would be Kyle's grandfather, Bill, with that huge smile, even after we just got it handed to us and played awful. He would just look at me with that smile and say, "Don't worry, DC, you'll get 'em next time." My response could only ever be to just smile back no matter how aggravated I was about our performance. Again, what made it even more special, was the sincerity with which he said it to me. He truly believed that we would get them next time. He always helped me keep things in perspective.

After Bill passed away, I sent an online condolence through the funeral home web site to the family and couldn't help but mention how I always remembered Bill's huge smile and how it could light up a room. The funeral attracted one the largest crowds that I had seen at a funeral for someone Bill's age. I literally stood in line for over an hour before getting to the casket to view Bill. Even more proof of the positive energy that Bill transmitted to those that he had touched during his life. Once I finally got to the family and we exchanged hugs and tears, Marianne told me how much what I had written about Bill had meant to her. I simply replied that it was from the heart.

Kyle, his wife, Angie, and Rick and Cozy all told me that it really meant a lot to them that I had taken the time to attend. In my mind, there was no choice. Bill deserved for me to be there. So did the rest of the family; not attending was not an option in my mind.

Then came the defining moment, Cozy introduced me to another member of the family. I can't remember anymore if it was an aunt or sister or someone else, but what Cozy said hit me like a ton of bricks. She said, "This is DC, he was Kyle's baseball coach forever. He and Dad had a special connection; they are both positive energy people. Dad never wanted to have any part of negative energy so he and DC had an immediate connection because DC was the same way, always positive. Dad always thought highly of DC."

To say I was touched was an understatement. Here the man that I had pulled positive energy from also pulled positive energy from me. It was also eye-opening for me and became the defining moment that I mentioned because I had lost that positive energy in 2010 and the results spoke for themselves.

You see, as I mentioned before, 2010 was not my best year as a coach. I started the year with a very positive outlook on the season. Since 2002, I would literally coach about 120 to about 140 baseball games a year. I would coach our college-age team in the summer and then one of our youth teams in the fall. Since 2003, I have coached our 16-U team in the fall. So for the college guys in the summer we had a very good team on paper going into the season. However, this season, we ended up underperforming like I'd never seen before. We got off to a really slow start and never really ran on all cylinders as a team. We lacked leadership and team chemistry; the largest lack of leadership came from the top, me. I'm man enough to admit that and will take that responsibility squarely on my shoulders. Our organization grew considerably in 2010 and I allowed those off-field distractions to affect my coaching on the field. As I mentioned earlier in the book, I have always loved coming to the ballpark. That didn't really change in 2010, but there were times when it became a grind and I am sure that my players could sense that. In turn, because I lacked focus and concentration, so did they. Some coaches have no idea how much your players feed off your energy as a coach. Without ever speaking a word, people can sense the mood that you're in. I'm convinced that my players could sense that I was distracted in 2010 and that carried over into their performance on the field.

Everything I did that helped make me a successful baseball coach for twenty-one years I lost sight of in 2010. All of the stuff that I said I did in the beginning of this book, I allowed myself to get away from in 2010. I felt the pressure of our organization's growth, and with very little help from our board in helping to manage that growth, I allowed that pressure to reflect in how I approached the game. Again everything that I mentioned earlier in the book that made me successful for twenty-one years, I didn't do.

I stopped smiling, I was stressed, and that stress showed. The positive energy that Cozy had spoken about was gone. Instead of showing up at the baseball field being my release for stress as it had been for so many years before, it was now another source of stress.

Our summer team finished the season with a record of 30-27-2, losing for the third straight year in our league semifinals of the play-offs. At the conclusion of the season, I immediately announced that I was stepping down as coach of that team. Some had thought that it was a knee-jerk reaction, but I had actually made the decision to step down around the middle of our season. To take things from bad to worse, once I had made my mind up that this was going to be my final year, I couldn't wait for the season to end. This was something that I never would have thought that I would experience in my life, literally wanting a baseball season to end.

When the summer season ended on a Friday night, my fall season started the following Monday. I was actually really looking forward to the start of our 16-U fall season. In my mind, I thought that this was what I needed, a change of scenery so to speak, a fresh start, a fresh look, new players, everything would be great. The only problem was that even with a change of scenery, a fresh start, a fresh look, and new players, the one thing that didn't change for the 2010 fall season was me. I was still stressed, I still wasn't smiling, and I was still showing up at the baseball field with it being another source of stress instead of being my release for stress as it had been for so many years before. It was taxing to say the least.

Another one of the many wisdoms that my mother had taught me in my life was that you can never run from yourself. You can change jobs, you can change cities, you can change spouses, but if you're the problem and you don't change yourself, it really doesn't matter who you're with or where you go; the same problems will continue to surface if you don't fix the real problem, which in many cases, is within you. This was something that she used with drug addicts, to get them to admit that they were responsible for their actions, but drug addicts oftentimes aren't the only people who need to take responsibility for their own actions. We all need to. She once again proved to be right in 2010, five years after her death; she was still teaching me life lessons. My attitude was the problem that caused our summer team to not succeed in 2010 and I was also the problem that caused our 16-U team to have such a horrible season in 2010 as well. Sometimes you just have to be man enough to look in the mirror and determine if you really like what you see.

On top of all that, our 16-U team was not very good. We were going to struggle no matter what in 2010. To begin with we were very young, twelve of the fourteen players on the roster were fifteen years old. We knew that going in and I really did think that we could overcome that. We had some talent, but we also had some players who really struggled to compete. My hope going into the season was that we could get the players who were not as talented as some of the others to work hard and rise up to play at a higher level. With a better coach, that would have happened, with me at the helm in 2010, there was no hope of that happening. In most seasons, my positive outlook and energy would help get my players to perform at a high level, many times a level that was really higher than they should have been competing at. A good coach can get more out of his players than they would ever expect to get out of themselves.

Energy, whether it's positive or negative can easily be picked up from other beings. Whether it's a dog or a human or something else, we all have somewhat of a sixth sense that other beings can draw off you. They may not actually know that they are getting those vibes from you, but they certainly will affect how you relate to them and how they respond to you. Positive energy draws positive results; negative energy draws negative results.

So going into the 2010 fall season with some very young players and with some players who lacked talent, we needed to rely on our team chemistry to be successful. This once again, was going to be a tall task considering we had zero team chemistry. Our two best players literally hated each other and this just continued to manifest itself throughout the season. We had no direction. When mistakes were made, we decided the best option was to point fingers at our teammates as opposed to picking each other up. I said all of the things that I had always said in the past, but these players just weren't buying into it.

Again, the problem was me. Even though I was still saying all of the things that I had always said in the past that my players would latch onto and buy into, I truly believe that their sixth senses took over; regardless of what I was saying, they knew that in 2010, it was only lip service. There was no substance and that was a glaring problem. When I was in sales, I would always tell my customers that I could never sell something that I didn't believe in. This was the problem here, I was saying all of the right stuff, but even at fifteen and sixteen years old, kids are pretty smart. They could tell that I didn't really believe what I was saying or, worse yet, that I didn't really believe in them. I tried early, believe me, I tried to make it happen and it just didn't, which compounded the problem. As the season went on, things went from bad to worse. I continued to have off-field distractions and they continued to overflow into my performance as coach, which then had a domino effect onto the players and their performance.

That lack of chemistry that we started the season with just manifested itself as the season went on. Our two star players that hated each other so much began to wear their emotions on their sleeves and created a divide among the team. Instead of the better players pulling the less talented players up to their level and leading by example, they allowed their frustration to get the best of them and actually lowered their level of play to that of the less talented players.

The team ended up going 17-35-2. In our organization, we always state that our main objective, as an organization, as a team, is that we're playing better baseball at the end of the season than we did at the beginning of the season. Stressing the fundamentals, we progressively get better as the season goes on. We didn't do that. We were playing worse baseball at the end than we did at the beginning, and we went 1-9-1 to finish the season and found new ways to lose baseball games down the stretch. We'd blow leads late, we'd come out flat and get our asses kicked right out of the gate and everything in between.

My composite record as a coach in 2010 was 47-62-4, one of my worst seasons ever, and there was no finger-pointing to be had. It was all solely on my watch and my shortcoming.

Our summer team should have won fifty games. We had one of the best teams that our organization had ever assembled "on paper" and with even a little bit of leadership, we should have won our fifth championship.

Our 16-U team in the fall, as I said was not the greatest on paper, but we certainly should have been a .500 team that season. Again as a coach, these young impressionable kids were looking to me for answers and I completely dropped the ball.

I let my team down and our organization down by allowing off-field distractions affect my performance in 2010.

Cozy's comment at the end of 2010 resonated deep within my soul and forced me to take a step back and look in the mirror. I didn't like what I saw. I had to get back to the roots that made me successful or things would just get worse.

Leaders need to lead; they cannot allow pressure and distractions to overwhelm them. That is what separates a leader from a follower. In 2010, I was far from being a leader; I had to take a step back, reevaluate what I was doing, and get back to my roots, foundation, and beliefs that had worked for twenty-one years of coaching.

I was determined after Bill's funeral to change and get back to being positive regardless of the situation. I worked hard over the winter and made a conscious effort to keep the positive energy flowing regardless of what happened.

Our organization continued its growth spurt as we entered 2011 and we certainly were not immune to our own growing pains. We had a solid core of good young coaches that came into the organization during the 2010 season and we were also making some drastic changes as an organization.

As president of the organization, I dedicated countless hours in the off-season to sit down and meet with all of our coaches and several of our parents to explain what Berkshire Baseball stood for as an organization. I was dedicated to separating the perceptions and reality of what our goals were.

We have posted our mission statement on our web site and in just about every single publication that we've ever printed, yet some people, within the organization and certainly outside of the organization, seem to draw their own conclusions as to what we stand for.

Our mission statement is pretty simple in my mind, it reads...

> The objective of the Berkshire Baseball Club is to promote amateur baseball at every level. Our organization shall strongly encourage our beliefs of good sportsmanship, honesty, loyalty, dignity, humility, class, and respect for authority.

> We will strive to teach and develop the necessary skills for our players and participants to reach the "next level," all the while fully realizing that for many of the players that go through this organization, the "next level" for them may very well be LIFE. Therefore, let it be known that it

is the responsibility of our members and coaches to not only teach and train the young individuals that participate in our program to be better ballplayers, but more importantly, to be better human beings.

To achieve this objective, the Berkshire Baseball Club will provide supervised baseball & softball programs for youth participants in conjunction with the rules and regulations of the local leagues and tournaments in which they participate as well as the official baseball rules.

This organization will operate as a non-profit 501(C)(3) entity."

The one thing that is not mentioned in that mission statement is the word "elite." However, 90 percent of the people who have an opinion on Berkshire Baseball, will tell you that they perceive our organization to be an "Elite Baseball Organization." I'm not sure where that comes from. We've never said that, we've never professed that, and we've certainly never believed that.

What we hang our hat on is that we're an old-school organization that stresses "*our beliefs of good sportsmanship, honesty, loyalty, dignity, humility, class, and respect for authority.*"

The second paragraph again, does not reference the term "elite" in any way, shape, or form. It simply states:

We will strive to teach and develop the necessary skills for our players and participants to reach the "next level," all the while fully realizing that for many of the players that go through this organization, the "next level" for them may very well be LIFE. Therefore, let it be known that it is the responsibility of our members and coaches to not only teach and train the young individuals that participate in our program to be better ballplayers, but more importantly, to be better human beings.

That second paragraph is something that seems to me and our board of directors to be a pretty simple concept. We've had twenty-seven players that have played in this organization that have moved on to play professional baseball. We've had thousands who have gone into society as better human beings and productive members of society because of the life lessons that they have learned because of this organization, something that has nothing to do with being an "elite" baseball player.

Now don't get me wrong, our organization plays every game to win, we just do not take a "win at all cost attitude." This seems to be another difficult concept for some people to grasp in this day and age. For whatever reason, in our society today, people can't seem to understand how you can play to win while also teaching kids a life lesson. Life itself is about overcoming failure, learning from your mistakes, getting knocked down and then getting back up, wiping yourself off and learning from what just happened and becoming stronger because of it. There really are people out there who think that failing is not an option and that you have to win all of the time, now that's certainly not a reflection of life. Life is not easy, life is hard, there is nothing handed to you in the game of life, you have to work every day, every minute to be successful.

Vince Lombardi used the phrase, *"Strive for Perfection, Achieve Excellence."* Truer words have never been spoken. That is what life is all about; we live in an imperfect world, which is the harsh reality of life. We're never going to be perfect, and there will never be a team in Major League Baseball that goes 162-0. However, we all as human beings can always strive for perfection, knowing that it is an unrealistic goal and that we'll never be able to achieve it. Therefore, if through our efforts to strive for perfection, we achieve excellence, we have succeeded.

Our organization's tag line has been "Tradition of Excellence," not "Tradition of Perfection." There is a philosophy as to why we use that tag line, because perfection cannot be achieved. Excellence can be achieved. Vince Lombardi said it best, *"Strive for Perfection, Achieve Excellence."* That is always our goal as an organization.

So with all that being said, as I entered 2011 with the revelation that I needed to get back to my roots and emulate a more positive energy, I also needed to make sure that everyone who was representing our organization was on the same page in what we stood for and the principles that our organization was built on.

That process meant that we may have to say good-bye to some coaches, which we did. The biggest obstacle in running a large organization is managing the adults; the kids just want to play baseball and have fun, and it's the adult coaches and adult parents who generally have unrealistic expectations as to the child's reasons for playing the game in the first place.

As the season went on, one thing that was proven is that no matter what people say to you in noncompetitive setting, you really do not see their true colors until that first pitch is thrown.

Several coaches and parents who we thought "got it," didn't even come close to getting it and were forced to take a step back again at the end of 2011 and make sure that our pieces in the puzzle were the right pieces in the puzzle. We've also accepted the fact that this will be an ongoing process every year. It's part of the evolution of an organization and part of the evolution of life. You can never get complacent, you can never take a day off, you have to constantly be looking at yourself and reevaluating what you're doing and how you're doing it in order to stay at the top of your game. That goes for how you approach the game of baseball as a player, a coach, an administrator, but most importantly, how you approach the game of life as a human being.

You have to realize that that mirror hangs on the wall for a reason and regardless of where you go, it's always going to be that same person staring back at you every day and every night. There is only one way to change it if you don't like what you see and that's to be honest enough to change yourself.

I had to take a good hard look in that mirror at the end of 2010 and was man enough to realize that I didn't really like what I was seeing. I had to get back to my roots; I had to dig deep and pull that positive energy and stay focused on the positive.

The next year, 2011, was a test of that positive energy again, with the size and growth of the organization. It will always be a test because, as I said earlier, no matter how well you try to educate them, some people simply will not understand what we stand for; you always have to strive to get those right pieces in place in order to stay successful.

CHAPTER 18

What Is Your Legacy

So after twenty-three years of coaching baseball and counting, I start to sit and reflect at times as to what I may have accomplished in my life. I am certainly not that old. I am still a very young man, in my early forties. I hope I have many more years in the game ahead of me. But I still take some of those moments and sit back to reflect and think about what I've done and why I've done it.

I honestly have no complaints about the path that my life has taken up until this point. I have a wonderful

"Success is not determined by money or the things money can buy. It is not determined by trophies on the shelf or by the letters after one's name. Success is determined by one thing and one thing only: when you leave this earth, is it better because you were here?"

~Jim Dimick

wife who has stood by me through thick and thin. Our relationship has become stronger over the years because of the commitment and loyalty that we have for one another. She has allowed me to stay involved in a child's game, knowing that it helps keep me young.

I have four great children and eight wonderful grandchildren whom I am very proud of.

I could have stayed in sales and made a lot more money than I do by running a nonprofit youth baseball organization, I could have coached at the college level and made much more money as well, but at the end of the day, I know that I am right where I belong.

Regardless of the hours that I have put in over the years, it's very hard to ever look at what I do as work. It truly is a labor of love for me and I honestly can't think of anything that I would rather be doing.

I once heard someone say that if you love what you do, you'll never work a day in your life. I believe that to be true and feel fortunate that I can live it.

With that being said, when I look back over twenty-plus years of coaching, the easy stuff to see is already on paper. Somewhere on the Internet, the records, the league championships, the tournament championships, but as I've said so many times in this book, they are really the objects of the least substance during a coaching career or at least they should be.

The stuff of substance is much more difficult to measure. Sometimes you may never even see it in your lifetime.

I'm almost certain that Denny Werner, Dennis Blair, Bob Rentschler, and Barry Distasio had no idea the impact that they had on this young man's life, yet if they knew, or if those who are still living read this book, will they consider the impact on a young mans life to be one of their proudest accomplishments or the trophies and banners? I'm just one small chapter in each of their coaching legacies. There are thousands of other players out there who were influenced by those men during their coaching tenures as well, and that is the true legacy of their careers as coaches. What you have taught a young man or how you have influenced a young man's life is the true record of wins or losses in a coaching career.

One of the reasons that every coach loves to see his former players after their playing days are over is because it gives them a chance to see their legacy in action. They get a chance to see what type of human being they have become, what type of husband, what type of father, what type of businessman and what type of teacher.

It is seeing those seeds that you sowed so many years before, the feeling of a proud parent, which gives you a true sense of accomplishment in your life. When you see former players' successes, you can only hope that something that you had taught to them while they played for you helped them to achieve the successes that they're now experiencing.

Every once in a while, you are fortunate enough to see it firsthand, to see one of your players come back and coach and hear him passing on one of the lessons to his players in his own words that you taught him.

Many people have different reasons for getting involved in coaching in the first place. For me, as I said earlier, I was kind of thrown into it, coaching my peers at a very young age. But after the initial shock, I was determined that if I was going to continue to coach, I was going to do it right and for the right reasons. As I began to teach and coach young people, I took that responsibility very seriously, knowing that I had a huge impact on their young lives.

Being around these young men and teaching them life skills through the game of baseball helps to keep me young at heart. It keeps me energized and it keeps me motivated. In a way, I guess that helps me deal with my own mortality. We all know that we will not live forever, but perhaps if something that we teach a young man on the baseball field as it pertains to life can be passed on from generation to generation and live on forever, then maybe it makes us immortal in some way.

I often use a quote by the great Jackie Robinson, *"A life isn't significant except for its impact on other lives."*

It's a quote that is part of my signature block on every e-mail that I send and it's a quote that I take very seriously. It should hit home to every individual that has ever coached or taught young people. Just think about that quote, *"A life isn't significant except for its impact on other lives."* How powerful is that statement? When it comes right down to it, when we leave this earth, the only significance that our life has on this world is how we've impacted those that we came in contact with while we were here. That's it, nothing more, nothing less. That is our legacy, positive or negative, how we are remembered by those who we touched on earth is all that we have going for us.

If we as coaches really take that quote to heart, it should completely change the thought process in how we go about our everyday activities. Whether we realize it or not at the time, every comment that comes from our mouth, every action on the field and off is being digested by those young lives that we are around day in and day out. They are sponges, they take it all in, and they take it in even when they do not realize that they are taking it in.

When I was eight, I never thought of Coach Distasio's comments to me as a defining moment of my life, but they were. In 1978, I may not have been able to tell you that those simple words would be replayed in my mind thousands of times throughout my lifetime, but they have been and more than likely will continue to be.

You never know when something that you say or do to one of your players will turn into a defining moment for an individual so be sure that you take every action and every comment very seriously.

I guess in the end, we never will know what our legacy will be or was and it is very possible that it is different for every player that we've ever coached.

I can only hope that somewhere along the way, some of the players that I have coached over the years will someday say, "I'd like to share with you something that my old baseball coach, Dan Clouser, once taught me..."

And that, would the greatest legacy that I could ever leave on this earth.

A final (unoriginal) thought to pass on...

THE COACH

The coach is a politician, a judge, a public speaker, a teacher, a trainer, a financier, a laborer, a psychologist, and a chaplain.

He must be an optimist, seem humble, and yet be very proud; strong, but at times weak; confident, yet not over-confident; enthusiastic, but not too enthusiastic.

He must have the hide of an elephant, the fierceness of a lion, the pep of a young pup, the guts of an ox, the stamina of an antelope, the wisdom of an owl, the cunning of a fox, and the heart of a kitten.

He must be willing to give freely of his time, his money, his energy, his youth, his family life, his health, and sometimes even life itself. In return, he must expect little financial reward, little comfort on earth, little privacy, and little praise, but plenty of criticism.

A good coach is respected in his community, is a leader in his school, is loved by his team, and makes lasting friends wherever he goes.

He has the satisfaction of seeing youth develop and improve in ability. He learns the thrill of victory and how to accept defeat with grace. His associations with athletes help keep him young in mind and spirit; and he, too, must grow and improve with his team.

In his heart he knows that, in spite of the inconveniences, the criticism, and the demands on his time, he loves his profession, for his is THE COACH.

~Author Unknown.